May God
richley bless
your health
and your journey!

Frank Curless

Pursuing the Heart of God

*One Man's Story of Healing
and Restoration*

Frank Curtiss

Frank Curtiss

An Intellect Publishing Book
www.IntellectPublishing.com

Copyright 2023 Frank Curtiss
Cover Art by Theodora Henderson
ISBN: 978-1-961485-15-0

First Edition: September 2023
FV-4HB

Inquiries to: info@IntellectPublishing.com

Contact the Author:

Frank Curtiss
11744 158th Ave. NE
Redmond, WA 98052
C: 425-269-3909

Email: curtissliterary@gmail.com
www.frankcurtiss.com

Dedication

This book is dedicated Joel and Jenna Curtiss,
the two children who left too soon.
My heart will swell and throb with joy when
we see each other again in heaven.

Pursuing the Heart of God

One Man's Story of Healing and Restoration

Frank Curtiss

Introduction:

"Lovers of truth follow the right path because of their wonderment and worship of God." Proverbs 14:2 (TPT).

This book is a love story, the story of how Jesus took me from a broken man to a man made whole by his Holy Spirit. He accomplished this by his incomparable comfort and by showing the depths of his beauty. He has put his heart in me, a heart that now passionately burns for his presence.

This is not a book to tell you how you should live your life. There are enough books out there that will tell you that if you follow their paths, your life will be wonderful. Good luck with those. I've never been one to tell anyone how to live. I would much prefer to inspire in some way, or say some small thing that gives you more courage to continue down life's journey with God, and to find a deeper level of intimacy with Jesus.

Why am I Writing this Book?

In the book of Hebrews, the Word of God tells us:

"And let us consider how we may spur one another on toward love and good deeds, not giving up meeting together, as some are in the habit of doing, but encouraging one another—and all the more as you see the Day approaching." Hebrews 5:11 (NIV).

The Passion Translation (TPT) says it in a unique way:

"Discover creative ways to encourage others and to *motivate them toward acts of compassion, doing beautiful works as expressions of love."*

My story is one of grave mistakes, near-crippling adversity, and crisis of faith. But more than that, it is a story of God's hand at work in the midst of it all. He has done a work in our lives that only he could do, binding up broken hearts, restoring shattered trust, renewing hope, and turning our ashes into joy. For only he satisfies the deepest longings of our soul. I hope that by telling my story, that your heart, too, will yearn deeply for more of him.

So, in line with God's plan, I hope to encourage you, the way so many have encouraged me. We need one another. That is why he tells us *"not to give up meeting together."* We all face adversity in our lives. And we are much better at overcoming our challenges together than facing them alone. God knew that.

I am sixty-nine years old as I begin this writing. Through my years I have learned some things. We all do. I would like to think I have gained some wisdom. We are meant to seek after it. If you don't believe me, read Proverbs. But God also tells us in Proverbs, *"Don't be impressed with your own wisdom."* Proverbs 3:7 (NLT).

I suppose this is part of humility. I have no problem with that because the more I come to know, the more I become aware of all that I do not. And anything I have to give does not originate from me. It is all a gift from God. Or as a friend recently said to me, "I can only give that which has been given to me."

A Unique Way of Storytelling:

This book is about God, and my journey with him. In these pages you will find psalms and poems which I have written. They are part of our story, and things God has taught me along the way. I say "our" because my wife Rhonda and I recently celebrated fifty years of marriage—a miracle in itself—and so our stories, hers and mine—are inseparable. And yet we respond so differently to the things that this life, and God, bring our way.

The other reason I say "our" is because my (and our) story is intertwined with God's. You might think that an odd statement, but our stories are really "his story" acted out in us. Yes, what we know as "history" is really "his-story," for he created us and placed us in a time and place. And though we have free will—a key principle in our relationship with him—he is always there, ready to pick us up when we mess up. He constantly invites us to turn our hearts back toward him.

As you read forward, you will see that ours is not an easy story. Some of you will be drawn to the difficult part of the story because of your compassionate hearts. Others will find it difficult, possibly because it opens up some of your own wounds. Whatever the case, I hope the hard part does not scare you away from reading on. It is not intended to be the focal point. The heart of the story is one of God's pursuing love, his comfort, his healing, and his ability to redeem and restore. I hope to be able to show you, in psalms and story form, the essence of who God is to me—his glory, his beauty, his wonder, and his goodness. And why I worship and pursue him with my whole heart, even after all he has allowed me to walk through.

A Psalm: Yearning for God

Frank Curtiss, March 2002

What words do you have for me today?
My ears are open to hear your word
My heart yearns to commune with you
To see and hear the Holy One of Israel
To see your face, to hear your voice
To feel your touch, to know your heart
This desire burns deep in my soul

Anticipation of your holy presence

A gnawing hunger, unquenchable thirst

Which only you can satisfy

Come Jesus, hold me in your arms again

Envelop me in your wings of love

I am your sheep, waiting to hear your voice

I am your bride, awaiting your return

Come, Lord Jesus, I desire your presence

Do not delay, come today, come now

My Love for the Biblical Psalms:

I love the Psalms! I read one every night before I go to sleep. It settles my mind and heart after whatever stresses or difficulties I have faced that day. I call it *bookending* my day, because I also try to begin each day with a devotional time of reading his Word, journaling, worship, and prayer. I think it is the most important thing we can do as believers to mature in our faith and walk in the promises of God.

I love the Biblical Psalms because they are honest. The psalmists (not just David, there are several) are not afraid to lay it all out on the table … their fears, their doubts, struggles, sorrows, and hopes. They even have the nerve to challenge God: *"Where are you God?"* or *"Why, O God?"* Yet, even in their times of hopelessness and despair, they almost always turn to praise at some point. I believe this, too, is a healthy practice.

These attributes of the Psalms free me to live my life openly and honestly before God. I personally believe this is important for our faith. Don't try to put up a false front with God! Okay, I just broke my own rule and told you how to live your life. But trust me, he knows your every doubt, your every sorrow, your every point of contention with him, even better than you know them yourself. So why try to hide it? Live before him as an open book.

There are many examples of this in the Scriptures. Moses wasn't afraid to lay out his feelings before God, and even tell him when he thought he was being unfair. David did the same, as did Asaph, one of my favorite psalmists. And if you really want to see gut-level honesty, read Lamentations, chapter three, written by Jeremiah.

One other thing I love about the Psalms is the way they reveal the heart of the Father. We learn about his compassion, his mercy, his faithfulness, as well as his righteous judgments. He is portrayed as a rock, a fortress, our strength, our shepherd, and our dwelling place. And we learn that he is *"Perfect in beauty,"* and *"Robed in majesty."*

A few months ago, I taught a class at our church about writing psalms. As part of it, we discussed the Biblical Psalms, because I wanted to use those as our model. Here is something I wrote and read aloud on the first evening:

The Psalms: An Intimate Reflection of Life …

Frank Curtiss, December 2022

A place where you find your own story
In them we discover …
… How to live, Open and Unafraid before God
From them we learn WHO God is …
And who he is not
The Psalmists wrote about the Past ….
The awesome works of God
And prophesied about the Future
They foretold to us … Jesus
Even before we met him in the flesh
How he would suffer … and ascend to his throne
So, we might live in abundance …

Even as we walk through the valley of death
They show us how to love God …
And love those around us …
And who and what to hate
They expressed courage … and fear
How to live as a warrior …
And how to be a lamb led to living water
They help us express our joy …
And embrace our lament … our sorrow
They bring us comfort
They are Open and Honest
Unafraid of what man thinks
They expressed hope and trust …
In God … in eternity … in his promises
Even as they openly admitted their doubts
And questioned the very God who created them …
Not always in a reverent way
"My God, my God, why have you abandoned me?"
Without fear of being honest with Yahweh …
Though they feared Him
So, they repented of those doubts
And their many other sins
But more than anything, the Psalms are prayers
They teach us how to pray
Openly and Honestly before God
With hearts wholly abandoned to his will
Trusting in his deep, abiding love

I will write more about the Biblical Psalms throughout this book. If you want to delve deeper, there is a book I highly recommend titled, *Open and Unafraid: The Psalms as a Guide to Life,* by W. David O. Taylor.

The Word of God:

I love God's Word! More and more, I've come to see it as my Father speaking directly to me (and all of us, of course). I'm learning to take him "at his word," so to speak. I used to have a hard time with some of the Old Testament stories, such as the story of Jonah. Then, one day our pastor pointed out that Jesus himself validated these stories by the references he made to them. That settled that. At least it did for me.

In this book, I will often quote the Scriptures. You've probably already noticed my use of different translations. When I come to verses that are either confusing or particularly meaningful to me, I often look at them in several translations, searching out the deepest understanding possible. Sometimes I prefer the way one says it better than the others, even though they are saying the same thing. I hope it does not offend you that my quotes come from a variety of translations. I will only quote them if I believe them to be accurate. I will note the translation used in parentheses. If uncertain what the initials mean, there is a footnote in the final pages of the book.

On another note, I will often substitute the name Yeshua for Jesus. Jesus is simply the English translation of the name Yeshua, which is the Hebrew name for Jesus. Both carry the same meaning, "salvation." I hope you don't mind my switching them up. I am becoming more and more fond of using the name Yeshua.

Before we move along, here is one of my favorite Biblical Psalms. I have removed the verse numbers so you can read it the way it was written. I love the imagery. If I ever write anything this beautiful, I will feel blessed indeed:

Psalms 42 (NIV)

For the director of music. A maskil of the Sons of Korah.

As the deer pants for streams of water,
so my soul pants for you, my God.
My soul thirsts for God, for the living God.
When can I go and meet with God?
My tears have been my food day and night,
while people say to me all day long, "Where is your God?"
These things I remember as I pour out my soul:
how I used to go to the house of God
under the protection of the Mighty One
with shouts of joy and praise among the festive throng.
Why, my soul, are you downcast? Why so disturbed within me?
Put your hope in God, for I will yet praise him, my Savior and my God.
My soul is downcast within me;
therefore I will remember you from the land of the Jordan,
the heights of Hermon—from Mount Mizar.
Deep calls to deep
in the roar of your waterfalls;
all your waves and breakers have swept over me.
By day, the LORD *directs his love,*
at night his song is with me—a prayer to the God of my life.
I say to God my Rock, "Why have you forgotten me?
Why must I go about mourning, oppressed by the enemy?"
My bones suffer mortal agony as my foes taunt me,
saying to me all day long, "Where is your God?"
Why, my soul, are you downcast?
Why so disturbed within me?
Put your hope in God, for I will yet praise him,
my Savior and my God.

Why I Write Psalms:

In my journal in July 2002, I wrote: "My purpose is to live as a man after God's own heart, showing his love and compassion to those around me; and live my life as an inspiration to myself and others."

I began to write psalms more than twenty years ago. There were reasons I began, and reasons I continue. I needed a way to communicate with God, a way to be honest with him the way David and the other psalmists were. I found that my prayer life lacked focus and honesty. My mind would skip from here to there like a stone skipping across the water. But when I put pen to paper, I became more engaged, and the deepest thoughts of my heart began to emerge. It became a way for me to process my thoughts and emotions. I learned more about myself, and I learned more about God, for it also gave me a way to hear his voice. And it gave voice to my thankfulness and praise. Even when my heart wasn't in it.

I will explain more about my reasons in a later chapter, but I have one more thing to say about this for now. When I refer to my writings as psalms, I am in no way comparing them to the Divine Word of God as written in the book of Psalms or other parts of the Bible. I am keenly aware of what the writer of Proverbs 30 related when he wrote, "Do not add to these words."

Yet, I do feel inspired by the same Holy Spirit that inspired David and others to write those found in the Book. I am a believer in what is known as the "rhema" word of God. Rhema refers to the *spoken word*. It also refers to *fresh revelation*. I am sure you have experienced it. Think of those times when you were reading the Bible and suddenly a verse which you've read many times suddenly jumps off the page at you. You finally understand what God is saying to you. Another example is when you are spending time with God in meditation or prayer and you hear the quiet voice of the Holy Spirit speak something to your heart for yourself or for another.

There are a couple of cautions here. First and foremost is that the *rhema* word must always be consistent with the *logos*, the written Word of God. If in doubt, it is always best to share it with a pastor or other spiritual leader whom you trust.

Here is another of my early psalms:

A Psalm: You are Mighty

Frank Curtiss, May 2, 2001

Lord, I praise you for you are mighty
You protect your servant before and behind
You wipe away all the tears from my eyes
After a dark night, you bring joy in the morning
Your ways are beyond my understanding
Your thoughts higher than my thoughts
You love me without good reason
You bless me though I deserve to be cursed
You discard my sins into the great sea
You make my robe white by your own blood
For my sake you wore a crown of thorns
I can never repay your awesome sacrifice
Nor do I deserve such great mercy
Help me to understand the depths of this love
Help me to see my place in your heart
Place in my heart your compassion and mercy
Give me strength to walk upon this path
The path you've placed my feet upon
Walk with me and show me which way to go
That I might bring glory to you
Selah

The Power of Story:

Now I would like to talk about the power of story, and why I am choosing to share some of mine. I say *some*, only because it would take me twenty books to tell it all.

We all have a story. And it is in stories that we learn how to live. God knows this. I believe that is why most of the Bible is written in story form. We read the stories of the saints of old and we see what they did well, when they walked in faith and obedience to God; and we see when they failed, miserably at times. And we learn from it all. Much of the New Testament is also written in story form, especially the gospels and the book of Acts.

And Jesus presented the Kingdom of God in stories. He told story after story about kings and vineyard owners, fathers and sons, seeds being sown, and coins that were lost. We call these stories parables. They usually start out with "The Kingdom of God is like …." Jesus knew the power of stories. They helped the people understand. My favorite of these is the parable of the prodigal son. It illustrates God's heart in a way we would never understand if he simply tried to explain it to us.

Yes, we love stories. As I'm writing this, I'm sitting in a Starbucks in a Barnes and Noble for a change of scenery. As I made my way to the restroom, it occurred to me that the shelves here were filled with thousands of stories, both real and fiction. We learn from both. Now, it's my turn to tell you mine. I hope it will strengthen you in some small way.

PART ONE:
DEEP CALLS TO DEEP

"My deep need calls out to the deep kindness of your love. Your waterfall of weeping sent waves of sorrow over my soul, carrying me away, cascading over me like a thundering cataract." Psalm 42:7 (TPT).

Chapter One: Almost Calling it Quits

Here is another of my earliest Psalms.

A Psalm: My Heart's Desire

Frank Curtiss, November 2000

Lord, I desire to be a man after your own heart
Give me a heart like that of your servant David
Bless me with a heart to love you like that
I choose to praise you though my heart is downcast
I know my feelings are not to be trusted
But in you O Lord I can place my trust
For you love me with an everlasting love
Lord, help your love to flow through me
Make me a well from which others may draw living water
May I always feel your presence within
Let your love be my warmth on a cold winter day

I've been planning to write this book for a long time. After retiring from decades as a restaurateur, I took up writing a series of mystery novels set in Italy. I love Italy, the beauty of the place, the people, and of course the food. And I love writing these books. It's great fun. I get to exercise my creativity, allowing my imagination to run wild. I hope that as I age, writing will help keep my mind sharp. I doubt I'll ever get rich from it but that's not why I do it.

I decided to take a break from my series to write this book. I believe God wants me to. He placed the idea and desire in my heart. If it were not so, I think I would call it quits. It's been far more difficult than I anticipated. I didn't count the cost very well before I began.

Foolish me! I thought it would be easy. Much of what you'll find here, I've already written. I have written hundreds of psalms, including many that I really like. I also wrote a book called *A Father's Sorrow*. I never published it. I made a feeble attempt, but in hindsight I believe its true purpose was for me to process my sorrow. When I considered writing this book, I thought it would be easy to pull these materials together and add some about my recent journeys with God and all he has been teaching me. I was wrong.

I had not considered the cost of grappling with certain emotions again. As I began this task, I pulled out journals I'd kept from as far back as 2000. As I pored through these, looking for some of the early psalms I'd written, I found myself deep in a valley once again, face to face with my accuser. I've spent more than my fair share of time in those dark valleys. At first, I felt all alone there. But then God reminded me that he was always there with me, even when I couldn't see him. He took me by the hand, led me out of the darkness, and set my feet in high places. Sure, I revisit them from time to time—usually for brief periods of time—but now he was inviting me back. I found myself on the edge of a precipice, looking down. My courage began to fail.

Thankfully, if there is one thing I've done well in this life, it is cultivating friendship. I have more close friends than I have time to devote to them (a wonderful problem to have!). As I realized just how difficult this journey was becoming, I called upon them to pray. I know that they did because they are compassionate and trustworthy men. Their prayers renewed my courage.

When I shared my struggle with them, one of them spoke a few simple words to me … "You are saying that you believe God wants you to do this. That's all you really need to know." I knew he was right and it gave me the courage to forge ahead.

If you are a reader of God's Word, you are probably aware that Jesus also prays for us (Romans 8:34). I sensed his prayers a couple of mornings later, during one of these difficult times. In the course of my daily Bible study, he brought me to Isaiah 41:10:

> *"Don't be afraid, for I am with you. Don't be discouraged, for I am your God. I will strengthen you and help you. I will hold you up with my victorious right hand."* (NIV).

Two days later, he brought me to Isaiah 43:2, and the first part of verse 3:

> *"When you go through deep waters, I will be with you. When you go through rivers of difficulty, you will not drown. When you walk through the fire of oppression, you will not be burned up; the flames will not consume you. For I am the LORD, your God, the Holy One of Israel, your Savior."* (NLT).

These words from God strengthened me in my time of need.

What I am dreading most are the next few chapters because that is where I lay out the really hard stuff—the things that are challenging to talk about. As I said in my intro, I hope you don't find it so difficult that you set the book aside. Because after that, I get to tell you the story of all the amazing ways God entered the picture and began his work of restoration, and a return to a life of hope and joy that only he could accomplish.

I'm sure by now you are wondering about what hard things I am referring to. Read on and I will tell you.

Chapter Two:
Born of Adversity

A Psalm: A Broken Wing

Frank Curtiss, March 2001

I praise you Lord, for your truth has healed me
My wing was broken but you stooped down from heaven
Touched me, in the deepest recess of my soul
You declared over me, *"Indeed you are free."*
Your breath became the air on which I took flight
You strengthened me and caused me to soar upward
High into the heavens, as an eagle soars at dawn
Bring my family along O Lord my healer
Let us fly together in beautiful formation
Let our wing tips touch as we fly to great heights

When I wrote this psalm, I was in a place of feeling God's healing touch. But I was also looking for God's help with my family. The years leading up to this had been extremely difficult. I'm going to get right to the hardest part of the story so you will understand what I am referring to. Then, I'll go back in time and tell you the story.

God blessed Rhonda and I with four children—three sons and finally a daughter—after we had given up the idea of receiving that blessing. As young adults, our youngest son and daughter chose to end their own lives. Our third son, Joel, took his life in 2004. Our youngest, and only daughter, Jenna, in 2012. These losses were devastating beyond my human ability to withstand.

Your first question is probably how could we ever survive such horrendous losses and move on with our lives? I will begin by saying that you never really get over losses of this magnitude. Not a day goes by that I don't have moments of sorrow.

And yet, I don't live there. God has accomplished the impossible in our lives—that which he promised in the first three verses of Isaiah, chapter 61. The first two verses are what Jesus read aloud in the synagogue regarding himself:

"The Spirit of the Sovereign LORD is on me,
because the LORD has anointed me
to proclaim good news to the poor.
He has sent me to bind up the brokenhearted,
to proclaim freedom for the captives
and release from darkness for the prisoners,
to proclaim the year of the LORD's favor
and the day of vengeance of our God,
to comfort all who mourn,
and provide for those who grieve in Zion—
to bestow on them a crown of beauty
instead of ashes,
the oil of joy
instead of mourning,
and a garment of praise
instead of a spirit of despair." Isaiah 61:1,2 (NIV).

God has done an amazing work of healing and restoration in our lives. It was not a quick or painless process. Grieving never is. And God did not promise that we would not grieve. What he did promise was to "bind up" our hearts, to comfort us, to create something beautiful from the ashes of our life, and to bring us to a place where we can praise him once again. But we play a role in that too. We have to give him access to our hearts, to let him do what only he can do. That is not an easy thing when your trust in him has been shattered in a million pieces.

The Years Prior:

I wrote the following psalm in 2002, during the difficult years which led up to the loss of our son, Joel:

A Psalm: You Refresh My Spirit

Frank Curtiss, August 2002

Lord, you bring life to me
You refresh my spirit in times of need
My love for you had grown cold
You took me through the valley to renew it
The dark valley brought fear
Thorns and briars tore at my flesh
The enemy stalked me there
He offered to lead me out
But I saw the path was wrong
Then you met me there
You cast your light upon a good path
I caught a faint glimpse of you
A glimmer of hope arose
Though I saw your path was not easy
Your path took many twists and turns
Sometimes it led me deeper into the valley
I clung to the hope, lest it disappear
Then you brought me to the river
You invited me in … I hesitated

You gently took my hand and led me in
The water was cool and comforting
For a moment, I was afraid again
Fearing I might drown
Then you showed me … I already had
I had drowned in your love and mercy
You lifted me from the waters
You set my feet on a solid rock
We sat a while and then you spoke
You showed me the purpose of this journey
That I might truly know you
And for you to place your heart within me
From there we walked on together
On this journey you have taught me many things
For now the path wanders above the valleys
I can look back and see from where I've come
I know more valleys lie ahead
I no longer fear them
It's not that I desire the pain
But the deeper experience of you drives me onward
For nothing in this world is better

Rhonda and I married in 1972. We were barely nineteen. Our first son, Chris, was born in 1975. Our second son, Noah, in 1978. In 1979 we moved from Orange County, California, to Woodinville, Washington, driving our VW bus. I am going to skip most of the story of the early years.

Our first son, Chris, was easy to raise. He was not a perfect kid but I don't know any who are. After that, our other three presented challenges beyond our capacities to handle. We were ill-prepared to cope with the trials we faced. It was easy enough when they were young. The difficult days arrived with their teen years.

We felt that Woodinville was a good community for raising a family. We attended church and taught them about God. Each of our children accepted Jesus during their childhood. They seemed happy and well adjusted. Rhonda and I were imperfect parents. If you have kids, I'm guessing you are too. But we loved our children deeply. We still do.

I will readily admit the failings I had as a husband. In the late eighties, Rhonda's and my marriage was in crisis. It was largely my doing. Of course, she made mistakes too, but mine were the kind most women would never forgive. I struggled with sexual sin and became unfaithful to our vows. These sins had been my Achilles heel throughout my teen and adult years. It was a struggle that continually tripped me up, and nearly caused me to toss in the towel on my faith. I could make excuses from my formative years—a broken home—an absent father—but I believe in accountability for our own mistakes. It is miraculous that Rhonda gave me a second chance.

I was a good father, the kind that made pancakes for our kids on Saturday morning, and played football and baseball with them. I read them books and prayed with them at night. I coached soccer and got involved with Scouts with our youngest. We went camping and took wonderful family vacations to visit our family in California. I could go on, but suffice it to say that I loved my kids and wanted to be the father mine was not. This was true of Rhonda, as well.

But I know that my dalliances—which nearly wrecked our marriage—also caused me to be less than fully invested in my children at times. It didn't help that I had to do a fair amount of traveling with my job. In the late eighties I was a field consultant with McDonald's Corporation, which took me to Alaska and around the Northwest. It put a great deal of stress on Rhonda, and

I was at the peak of my struggles with being the husband and father I should be. I gave serious consideration to leaving her.

Thankfully, I came to my senses! After a great deal of soul searching, I decided that what I had was what I truly wanted. I recommitted myself to my marriage and to my children. In the process, I also took a long, hard look at my faith. I decided that it, too, was something I wanted to salvage. With God's help, I repented and chose him all over again. I re-enlisted, so to speak. When I did so, it was with a greater level of maturity. I had counted the cost. I knew it was worth it. God had proved himself faithful. He had never given up on me.

I wish I could say that my healing and transformation was easy and immediate. I had a lot of hard work ahead of me. I was a broken man in need of restoration. And my marriage was on life support. I had broken trust with Rhonda. She was deeply hurt and withdrew emotionally. I knew I had failed her. Now, all I could do was love her, prove myself faithful, and be patient.

The road to recovery is never a straight line. It takes you around blind curves, up hills and through valleys. Sometimes you are in a good place and can look back and take joy in where God has brought you from. Other times the path takes you into deep valleys where it's hard to see. In the months and years that followed, I vacillated between hopefulness to despair. I have always considered myself an optimistic person, but now the very core of the man I thought myself to be was being challenged.

At times, that road became very lonely. As Rhonda and I were in the process of rebuilding our marriage, our kids began to enter their teenage years. When your children are young, they look up to you. Now those days were disappearing, and there was a chasm of my own doing between Rhonda and me. The years ahead became so difficult at times, that we wanted to cry (and sometimes did). Thankfully, we had a good church and many wonderful friends to support us. Without them, we would have drowned.

As our youngest three entered their teen years, they entered a season of immense struggles and rebellion. For our boys, it did not begin until age sixteen or later. For our daughter, our youngest, it began even earlier. Alcohol and drugs played a role, and our relationship with them became extremely challenging. Mental health issues played a part, something we were slow to recognize. Bipolar disorder was one problem that caused erratic behavior, especially in Jenna. She acted out more than any of them. We tried everything, including counseling and tough love. Nothing worked. It was a scary time. After she made more than one attempt at running away, we decided to put her in a school for at-risk youth. It was heartbreaking.

In 1993, I left my job with McDonald's, and Rhonda and I opened our own restaurant: Frankie's Pizza and Pasta, a family Italian restaurant in Redmond, Washington. One significant advantage of this change was that I was now working with my family. No more travel. It put me in a place of accountability. Our two oldest sons worked for us from the beginning and, eventually, our two youngest as well. We had many good years there.

As part of our daughter's program for at-risk youth—we parents went through our own program—a series of seminars designed to teach us better parenting skills. They taught us about accountability and how to work together as a parental team, something we had never done very well. They were extremely helpful and God used them to mature Rhonda and I, and to bring us closer together. Our marriage was beginning to heal.

Chapter Three:
From Joy to Sorrow

"O Lord have mercy on me in my anguish. My eyes are red from weeping; my health is broken from sorrow." Psalm 31:9 (TLB).

A Psalm: Your Arms Surround Me
Frank Curtiss, February 2002

Lord, your word penetrates my soul
It transforms my heart
When I seek you I find you
Peace comes to dwell within
Where e'er I go you are with me
You hem me in before and behind
What more could I desire?
What in life could be better?
Than for you to walk beside me?
To be my constant companion?
My soul finds its rest in you
As I lean against your breast
Your arms surround me with love
With tenderness you hold me
The storms rage around me
I see them but they touch me not
I am safe and warm in your lap
Like a child I sigh happily

The magical child you created me to be
Is alive and well in your arms
Life is full of wonder again
A great adventure to be lived
The world is filled with your goodness
Why does it look so different
Beauty is everywhere to be seen
Green grass, blue skies, azure waters
'Tis because you've given me the heart of a child
And eyes to see what you see
I am happy

For over two years we saw little of our daughter. Our communication was letter writing and weekly phone calls. But those letters were a treasure. She remained rebellious at first, slow to embrace the structure of the program. But she was safe. Eventually, she began to work on herself. We did the same. She received her high school diploma there. The day she graduated from the program was one of the happiest days of my life.

After graduation, Jenna did really well for a time. We were so happy, so proud of her. But after a few months, the wheels began to come off again. When she turned eighteen, she decided that she didn't like the rules of living at home and decided to go and live with our second oldest son who had moved to San Juan Island in Puget Sound. Not long afterwards, she met a guy and they became serious. A few months later, they got engaged. Within a year, Jenna was pregnant. They moved back to Redmond and moved in with us. They got married, but sadly, things didn't go so well. He had a problem with alcohol and the marriage only lasted a year.

But one gift came out of it all—an amazing granddaughter! Teddy was born in the summer of 2004. Rhonda and I were at Jenna's side the night she gave birth. What unbelievable joy she brought to us! But our joy was to be short-lived.

Three months later, the unthinkable happened. Our third son, Joel, took his life. Let me tell you a little about him.

Joel's Story:

In the spring of 2003, Joel showed up at our house looking for a way to earn some money. He had been living in a very bad environment and wanted to go to San Juan Island to live with his brother and sister. His timing could not have been any better. Rhonda and I had just postponed a trip to Italy. We needed to be home to support Jenna during the difficult last days of her marriage. I had already scheduled the time off, so I decided to enlarge our back patio area with brick pavers. Joel and I spent the next two weeks laboring side by side. He worked hard. He was respectful, and we had some wonderful talks. Those days were a gift of epic proportions.

Joel was born with Asperger's syndrome, a form of autism (they no longer call it Asperger's, simply autism). We never knew that when he was growing up. We had never even heard of it. It wasn't until years later—when someone explained the symptoms to us—that the light bulbs went on. We finally understood what had been a mystery to us. It explained why he had been so different from his older brothers.

Joel struggled with social skills. He lacked confidence and was often withdrawn. For years we tried to figure out how to bring him out of his shell. We tried soccer and basketball. When sports did not fit, we tried scouting. It was like trying to fit a square peg in a round hole. We were at a loss.

In his late teen years, Joel began to drink. Eventually, that led into drugs. I believe one reason for this was it gave him more confidence in social situations. It gave him courage. It made him feel accepted.

But Joel had a brilliant mind. His math skills were exceptional (without even trying), and he loved music. We came to understand that those two things are connected. He learned to play the guitar and was very good at it but never wanted to perform. To spend time with him I used to invade his space and sit and listen to him play. His favorite thing to play was the introduction to "Wish You Were Here," a song by Pink Floyd. He played it beautifully. When we lost him, it became our grieving song. We listened to it over and over again. We even played it at his memorial service.

Though he had no desire to perform, Joel pursued his passion for music. He attended the Art Institute of Seattle and graduated with a degree in music production. He had a dream of making a career in the music industry but his life went sideways. He spiraled into a period of great difficulty. After a time, because of his choices, we had to ask him to move out. It broke our heart.

The story of his ups and downs after that is a long and complicated one, spanning a period of more than four years. He disappeared for a time. We didn't know if he was dead or alive. It turned out that he was living with a group of guys in the countryside who—rumor had it—were running drugs and producing lithium.

With the money Joel earned from helping to build our patio, he went to San Juan Island as planned. He moved in with his siblings but the roller coaster continued. He continued to make poor choices and later spent a few weeks in jail.

A few months after Teddy was born, he showed up at our door again. I have photographs of him holding her that I treasure. He told us he was going to California to follow his dream—to look for a job in music production. He spent a week sleeping on his brother's couch and we saw him a couple of times.

On Halloween night, his brother, Noah, told us he had left on a bus for California. He left without saying goodbye. We've often wondered if he knew what he was planning to do. Three days later I received a call from a detective in Long Beach, California. Joel had taken his life. He was twenty-three.

Joel was tall, about six foot three, and had long blond hair. He looked every bit the rock star. At his memorial, the thing we heard most from his friends was what a unique individual he was. He followed his own drum beat Though he went through many struggles, he was a gentle soul who never found his place in this world.

*****

A few months after the loss of Joel, I wrote this psalm:

A Psalm: Why do I Hold You at Bay?
Frank Curtiss, January 2005

Lord, I am desperate for you
Why do I hold you at bay,
  when my need for you is so great?
What do I fear?
My heart yearns for your love
So why do I not receive it,
  when you stand patiently,
  holding out your arms to me?
Lord, I thirst for you in this desert
I stand beside a spring of living water
  refusing to take a drink
What holds me back?
I think it is the pain that I fear
Serving you has cost me so much
And yet I have nowhere else to go
I am desperate for you
Cross the desert O Lord
Look for me like a lost lamb
Carry me home in your arms
I am lost. Come and find me

Chapter Four: No Words

"My soul refused to be comforted." Psalm 77:2
A Psalm of Asaph (NKJV).

No words can describe the pain of losing a child to suicide. It's a punch in the gut from which you cannot catch your breath. The hopelessness which had overtaken him now overtook us. Not only are you dealing with the grief of the loss, but you are trying to grasp the *why*. You have a thousand questions to which there are no answers. You try to understand, but you cannot. We would never have made it through these days if not for our family and friends whom God encircled around us.

I wrote the following poem a few months after we lost Joel.

A Poem: The Fighter
Frank Curtiss, January 2005

The punch came
From out of nowhere
Unseen
Unexpected
Knocking me to the mat
Dazed
Confused
I try to rise

Like a prize fighter
Fans cheer me on
They desire to see me rise up
In agony
I attempt to stand
Before the count of ten
My face bludgeoned
Vision blurred
I stumble about
A drunken man
No strength in my bones
Yet a fighter remains within
Nearly blind
Eyes swollen shut
I thrust about with fury
Looking for revenge
But upon whom
Do I land my blows?
For he who nearly
Knocked me out
Has exited the ring

Along with feelings of immense sorrow comes another feeling. I felt that I was a failure as a father ... that, somehow, I did not show Joel enough love, instill in him enough hope, teach him confidence, or a love for life. I questioned every choice I had ever made in regard to what kind of father I had been. Every mistake I ever made was magnified a thousand times.

My friends tried to reassure me. They told me over and over that I was a good father. It helped a little but not enough. After a time, I decided to see a counselor who specialized in working with survivors of suicide. It helped to be able to talk without being a continual burden on my friends. I learned a lot. One thing I learned was that family members of those who commit suicide are eleven times as likely to do the same. It brought me to my knees for my other children.

God used this counseling in my life. Little by little I stopped blaming myself. I helped the counselor re-start a suicide support group in our area which had fallen dormant. I remained in the group for about a year, until I felt it was time to move on. Counseling can only bring you so far. I needed God to do what he does best.

But there was a major hurdle to overcome. I was angry with God. How could he allow such a thing to happen? We had prayed and prayed during those difficult years. We've all heard the stories of how God miraculously intervened, preventing someone from taking their own life. Why hadn't he done that for my son? God was an easy target for my anger. My trust in him was broken—lying in a million pieces on the ground.

I did a lot of journaling in the days and weeks that followed, trying to process what had happened and honestly laying out my feelings before God. I can barely read them now. They are too raw.

In the beginning, my biggest struggle was that the question of my son's salvation weighed heavily on my mind. He had turned away from God. But one thing encouraged us. During his final visit with us, Joel had told Rhonda that he had begun to re-open the door to God. Over time, God made it clear to us that he had redeemed our son. Even in the midst of my grieving, I felt that I was hearing God's voice, reassuring my heart. Others—people whom I loved and respected for their faith— were hearing the same assurances. I'll share more on this later.

As I was wrestling with this—trying to find God's comfort— he reminded me of something Joel had shared with me. During the days Joel and I were together, expanding our patio, he shared a dream with me. I remember it like yesterday. We were in the car, headed to the hardware store when he told me that someday he wanted to move to a South Seas island and build a treehouse to live in, like the one in *Swiss Family Robinson*. It seemed sort of silly, but cool at the same time (I loved that movie!). Now I felt like Jesus was telling me that Joel was with him in paradise and that he was helping him build his treehouse. I still don't know if it was really God—or just my imagination anxiously looking for comfort —but it felt like something Jesus would do. Someday I will know.

A Poem: Reflections in Firelight

Frank Curtiss, March 2005

The fire casts its light
  as I sit and reflect
    upon days past
      many joyful, many sad
and I ask why?

Will I ever know?
Can e'er my heart
  find peace again?
For a fleeting moment I find it
Then returns the pain

That pain it is
  a part of me now
 I embrace it like a friend
But I loathe the guilt
  that does my heart rend

Chapter Five:
A Leap in Time

The following psalm was written three years after losing Joel. God was doing a good work in my heart, despite many challenges we continued to face:

Jesus, Heart of the Father

Frank Curtiss, October 2007

Jesus, my Jesus. My savior, my lord.
The very heart of the father
   is reflected perfectly in you.
God's great mercy to us
   was carried out in you.
Because you were obedient
   even unto death.
I fight and kick
At the suffering you bring.
And yet I know
   it is for your purpose
     that I suffer,
so, I may become like you,
   a man after God's own heart.
In you, I trust, O God.

Now, I am going to make a seven-and-a-half-year leap in the story. I want to get this out of the way.

On the first of April 2012, our only daughter, Jenna, followed in the footsteps of her brother. She was twenty-seven years old. Her daughter, Teddy, was seven. Our world came crashing down once again. How could such a thing possibly happen? I honestly didn't think I could ever recover.

Jenna's Story:

Jenna's story is a complicated one. Her path was quite different. After her divorce, her life continued its up and down cycles. She attended college, studying interior design, then dropped out. One day, at a low point in her life, she came to Rhonda and I and told us that she wanted to join the Army Reserve. She had already met with a recruiter.

She set up a plan for us to have temporary custody of Teddy. She entered the army, and headed to Georgia for basic training. Because Jenna had always struggled with authority, many in the family expected her to fail. She did not. In some ways it seemed to be exactly what she needed. Two months later, we flew to Georgia to attend her basic training graduation. From there, we drove her to Virginia where she was to enter training as a Chinook helicopter mechanic. She excelled. When she returned home, she was assigned to a Chinook helicopter reserve unit at Fort Lewis, Washington.

She did really well for a time. But the ups and downs were not over. She got into a relationship with a guy in her unit. They talked of marriage, but he wanted her to leave the army. She refused and they separated. She did not handle it well, and nearly took her life that day. Several people from her unit came to help in her time of crisis.

A few months later, her unit from Fort Lewis deployed to Iraq. Because of her near-suicide, they chose to leave her behind. But Jenna was not to be deterred. She had connections to the Chinook unit from Virginia, and one year later, when that unit shipped off to Iraq to replace the Fort Lewis unit, she was with them.

During the interim, Jenna had received additional training, and instead of serving as a mechanic, she became a crew chief on a Chinook helicopter, in charge of handling men and materials. She worked long, long, hours and served with honor. We missed her dearly. She was my girl. But my heart was proud and beginning to heal.

One summer day, I had a beautiful experience with God during my devotional time and wrote this poem based upon a verse in 1 Corinthians:

A Poem – Face to Face
Frank Curtiss, August 2008

"Now we see through a mirror dimly. Then we shall see face to face."
1 Corinthians 13:12 (ESV).

As my heart and mind
  quietly considered
  the things of God,
  the dim-mirror was shattered
  and for a moment
  I stood, face to face
  with Jesus.

You might think this to be
  a terrifying moment.
But oh, the opposite is true!
Let me tell you what I saw
  as I gazed into his face,
  the personal face of God.
My façade crumbled,
  as upon his olive-brow
  I saw the marks,

rough scars
where the thorns
had dug deep.
His nose was crooked
like a fighter
who had entered the ring
and taken a beating in my stead.
Some might consider
His face disfigured,
But what I saw…..
well, to me
it was the most beautiful face
I had ever seen.

Maybe it was the mouth
that I liked most,
the big smile
that drew me in,
sending warmth
through every fiber
of my new being.
Oh, what a welcome home
I felt in that!
Was he really that happy
to see me?
As if in answer
he caught my eye.
He'd been gazing deep
into mine all along.
I had been wrong.
His eyes were the best part.
Those dark sepia-pools

sucked me in.

My resistance
  quickly faded.
I was engaged,
  locked-in;
Knowing my soul
  and spirit
Lay fully exposed.
And yet,
  I felt no fear;
  no worry
  that a shadow of disapproval,
  or momentary flicker of incrimination,
  might cross his gaze.
For what I saw
  in those eyes,
  I can only describe as
  the sparkle of pure joy,
  fully revealing
  the deepest love,
  the warmest affection,
  my heart had ever known.

Jenna's Story Continued:

A year later we welcomed Jenna home. We were ecstatic. She was doing as well as we had ever seen her. We were so proud.

One day after she returned, she and I went to lunch and talked for hours. It was the best communication we had ever had. We talked about our relationship, and she shared her dreams and goals. She asked if she could return to work for us. At a low point in her life, we had fired her. Now, I was happy to give her another chance.

She returned to work, waiting tables, went back to college, and returned to her Fort Lewis Reserve unit.

One of the favorite memories of my life occurred a few months later. In October of 2010, Jenna ran in a half-marathon in the Bavarian town of Leavenworth, which lies on the eastern edge of the Cascade Mountains in Washington. It's a beautiful place, and was one of her favorites.

Rhonda, Teddy, and I waited anxiously at the finish line. As she crossed that line, Jenna had a look of tremendous strength and determination on her face. I was bursting with joy and pride. I have a photo of it that is a cherished possession. It gives me strength. We celebrated in town with bratwurst and beer.

But in the months that followed, things happened that sent Jenna into a period of great difficulty. One year after returning home, the Virginia Chinook unit that she had served with was redeployed to Iraq. They offered Jenna the chance to deploy with them but she wanted to complete her college. She chose not to go. A couple of months later, one of their choppers was shot down, killing everyone on board. Many on board, including the pilot, were her friends. In the days that followed, she was in communication with friends who had been on a following chopper and had watched helplessly as the first one went down.

Jenna attended the memorial service for the pilot, whose family lived about an hour south of us. She took it hard. Much harder than I understood at the time. Not only was she dealing with grief, but I believe she was dealing with survivor's guilt.

By then, Jenna's dream was to become a Chinook helicopter pilot. While serving in Iraq, a couple of the pilots had allowed her to fly in the cockpit with them. She was hooked. One of her strengths was her dogged determination. She worked and worked to get herself into pilot training school and was finally accepted. Weeks into the program, she was near the top of her class. Then, one day, she called home in tears. She had been kicked out of the program.

Someone reported that she had previously been on medication for her bipolar depression. Pilots are not allowed to be on any meds. She explained to us that, when she went for her physical, she told the doctor about it, and that he counseled her not to mention it again. It appeared that someone she knew, likely from her Fort Lewis unit, had reported this. She was devastated.

Jenna managed to get transferred from her unit at Fort Lewis to a PSYOP (Psychological Warfare) unit. She seemed to fit in well with them but never really recovered. She was struggling with extreme anxiety and PTSD. It had become worse after the loss of her friends on the Chinook chopper. She was drinking heavily and began to abuse anti-anxiety meds.

In addition to attending college, being in the Army Reserve, and waiting tables at our restaurant, Jenna had begun to work for the VA, the Veteran's Administration. She loved working with the veterans. She also went through Red Cross disaster training. When you look at someone with so many goals—so many aspirations and such purpose—you would not think them to be suicidal. A couple of weeks before she took her life, her unit went through a suicide prevention program. Suicide was, and still is, a major problem among military personnel and veterans, especially among those who have served in combat. Her commanding officer told us that he had been asked to rate the risk among those in his unit, and had not considered Jenna to be at risk. During this time, Jenna was also seeing a counselor at the VA. He told us that she had mainly been seeing him about relationship issues, something which had plagued her for years.

A few days before Jenna took her life, she was fired from her job at the VA for substance abuse. It was one more devastating loss. She had always seemed so strong. Time and time again she had been able to pick herself up after a major disappointment and move on. But not this time.

Jenna's life had been one of huge contrasts and contradictions. She was bigger than life. She was an adventurous woman. My head would sometimes spin as I watched her life. At one point, she even had a dream of becoming an MMA fighter (every father's dream!). A friend from her unit told us that she crammed more life into her twenty-seven years than most people did into a full lifetime. He was right. She was a warrior who had a soft, feminine side. She was athletic, but loved to cook and was very artistic. She loved people, and loved to serve them but struggled in her personal relationships, especially with men. She had faith but grappled with sins that often took her down. She was driven to achieve big things, yet there were times when she could barely pull herself out of bed. She was one of the bravest women I have ever known. But in the end, her courage failed her.

The army handled a big part of Jenna's memorial service. They honored her death as that of a fallen comrade. They gave her a gun salute as they would a soldier who had died in battle. It moved me to tears. But the moment that completely unraveled my heart was "the last roll call." One-by-one, her commander called out the names of soldiers who were present, to which they responded. Then, one last name was called … *"Private Curtiss … Private Jenna Curtiss … Private Jenna Christine Curtiss."* He explained afterward that this ritual is done to sear the memory of the fallen in the hearts and minds of their fellow soldiers, lest they forget. I don't imagine they ever could.

*****

The army provided a great deal of support to us. I respect them highly for that. Needless to say, we were devastated beyond our own ability to cope. Only God could restore us now. But once again my anger at him prevented me from going to the foot of the cross. For the third time in my life, I was in the middle of a crisis of faith.

A couple of months later I wrote the following in my journal:

Journal entry: June 18, 2012

God, let's talk. My heart does not trust you. I feel pain beyond my ability to bear. I am an emotional wreck. I have no confidence in prayer. You have answered few of mine; especially those most important to me. The price you've allowed me to pay is too high for me. And I have become bitter in my heart.

If you want me to walk with you, it will be up to you to heal my shattered heart, and comfort my spirit. And as far as faith goes — I have none. How will you ever overcome that within me? How will you?

A glimpse of heaven would be a good start. To see the smiling faces of those I love. Or maybe a visit from you, or one of your angels. Lord, manifest yourself to me.

Jesus, I am desperate for you. I know I have run from you. Pursue me. I know I have held you at arm's length. Wrap me up in your arms of comfort. I know I have let go of your hand. Catch me when I fall. I know I have been angry with you. Do not be angry with me. I know I have not been seeking you. Seek me. I have no faith in you. Have faith in me. Love me with an everlasting love.

*****

Later that summer, on a hot August day, we drove across the Cascade Mountains to hold an intimate family memorial in Leavenworth. We gathered in a quiet spot on a little island in the Wenatchee River which skirts the town. After a time of sharing memories, we scattered her ashes from a bridge into the swirling waters of the river. It was bittersweet. We headed into town and had bratwurst in her honor at the place where we had celebrated her half-marathon. Rhonda, Teddy, and I revisit these spots nearly every year.

PART TWO: BINDING UP THE BROKEN HEARTED

A Poem: All at Once

Frank Curtiss, July 2012

All at once
My heart was shattered
A thousand pieces lay upon the floor
Could it ever be mended?
Will it ever again be whole?
One by one
I gathered the scattered shards
and tried to piece them together again
Slowly, painfully it began to take shape
It never looked quite the same
Some pieces didn't seem to fit
Others were missing
Every now and then I'd find
a piece swept under the carpet
Or a friend would find
a piece I'd overlooked
Sometimes a piece would get stepped on
and further crushed
by some well-meaning soul
But after a time
it began to resemble a heart
It still ached a lot
Occasionally a sharp pain
would send it into spasms
Sending me in search
of some way to numb the anguish
But as the months passed

and the years became mist
The pain eased a little
My face was less contorted now
Joy crossed my path more often
And though my heart was still
a leaky, patched up vessel
it somehow seemed to function
as a heart is supposed to
Then came another blow
more crushing than the first
Despair washed over me
My old friend sorrow
pinned me to the ground
It seemed as if God himself
was out to crush me
and all his promises
were for naught
The pulverized pieces
were scattered like
black sand on the shore
pummeled by waves of sorrow
hope being towed under
by each receding wave
Swept away to the depths
like the ashes of my daughter
flowing down the river
to be embraced by the sea
I stumble about
feeling lost, helpless
knowing I could never

piece this heart together again
A question comes to mind
could these grains of sand
which I try to grasp
be melted in the refiner's fire?
Could they form a new heart?
I find myself wondering
what such a heart would look like?
Would it be Transparent?
Like a glass house? Wide open
for all the world to see?
all of my brokenness revealed?
Would it reflect God?
Of these things
I can only wonder
But there is a worry
that I have for such a heart
I fear that it might be
as delicate as crystal
and easily shattered again
And I ask myself
how much more sorrow
can a mere man take?

Is it humanly possible that my heart could ever recover from our losses? No. It is not *humanly* possible. It would take a miracle of God to put the pieces back together. In our case, it was a whole host of smaller miracles, each carefully orchestrated by God to recreate my heart and make it more like his.

Chapter Six:
The Beginnings of God's Comfort

"He will feed his flock like a shepherd. He will carry the lambs in his arms, holding them close to his heart. He will gently lead the mother sheep with her young." Isaiah 40:11 (NLT).

A Poem – Found By Him
By: Frank Curtiss, January 2009

I was found by him
Though I did not know it
Thinking all along
  It was I who discovered him
Believing myself clever
Smarter than those
  Who still groped about
But he just smiles
As a father with a young child
  Taking humor in my
    Misguided thinking
For as a lion stalks its prey
So I have been outwitted
It was, you see
From the very beginning

That he had planted the seed
 of himself within me
A yearning in my heart
And then as that lion
He pounced on me
At the most unexpected time

If you've had a difficult time reading the previous chapters, I understand. I know full well that we are not the only people in this world who have experienced deep grief. If we live many years, all of us will experience it at some time or another. There was a wonderful Czech woman who worked for us at our restaurant for nearly twenty years. When we lost our son and daughter, she honestly admitted to me that she had never lost anyone to whom she was close. A few years later, she lost three close family members at home in Czechoslovakia. All were unexpected, all in a matter of months. She was reeling.

But grief comes for many reasons, not just death. It can come from a health crisis—of our own or someone we love. Our hearts can be broken by the betrayal of people we love and trust, or loved ones struggling with addictions. There are more reasons than I can count.

As far as this book is concerned, the most difficult part of our story is now behind us. Now I get to tell the story of how God's miraculous interventions lifted us from the depths of despair and set our feet on high ground. This was no quick and easy process. Our grieving and restoration took years, and is still going on to this day. But God has brought us comfort, peace, and joy beyond my ability to comprehend. I will do my best to explain it, knowing all the while that some of it is unexplainable, except to say it is a mysterious work of his Holy Spirit.

One thing I've come to understand through all of this is the ability of joy and sorrow to coexist. Frankly, it surprised me. I had always considered them mutually exclusive, at least in their extremes. I was wrong.

There were times when the grief overwhelmed us, and times when we found great joy in our family, friends, and in unforeseen touches of God. We would laugh and cry at the same time. I first understood this dichotomy a few days after losing Joel. I was changing Teddy's diaper. She was three months old. As she fidgeted, fussed, and cooed, I looked at her with tears streaming down my face and talked to her like she could understand me … "How can a man be so happy and sad at the same time?" I asked her. I was truly perplexed. Both emotions were so strong within me.

I want to take a moment to talk about emotions. Feelings and emotions have gotten a bad rap in some Christian circles. Some say feelings can't be trusted. There is some truth to this. But we are going to experience them. It's inevitable. It is how we respond to them that is important.

God made us in his own image. He also has emotions. He experiences joy, anger, sadness, jealousy. He laughs, he cries, he loves … deeply, and he hates. I would list scriptural references but there are hundreds. The difference between God and us is that his emotions are always appropriate, always under his perfect control. They are sanctified. Part of our maturing—our becoming like him—is to let God sanctify our own emotions. This process is illustrated throughout the Bible, men and women known for their great faith who struggled greatly to balance faith in God with the way they felt inside.

Thankfully, in my own life God never condemned or chastened me for my emotions. Even in my anger, when I questioned his goodness, he was gentle with me. He carried me like a lamb, close to his heart.

If our first loss was crippling, the second was debilitating. I probably would have crawled in a hole and never come out again; but God had given us an important purpose in life, a reason to get out of bed in the morning. Her name was Teddy. She was seven years old when we lost her mom. Rhonda and I also had our two remaining sons to consider, as well as one another. We needed each other.

Even though I had purpose to move forward, my anger at God had come roaring back, and my trust and faith were shattered even more than before. I launched into a wrestling match with God of epic proportions. I refer to it as a wrestling match because of the story related in Genesis, chapter 32. The chapter describes the story of Abraham's grandson, Jacob, wrestling with an angel. Some say Jacob was emotionally bankrupt at this point in his life. God had made him promises which had not yet come to pass. After wrestling with him throughout the night, the man (later referred to as God) said, *"Let me go for it is daybreak,"* to which Jacob replied, *"I will not let you go until you bless me."*

God did bless Jacob, though he also touched his hip. Jacob had a limp for the rest of his life. Jacob literally wrestled with God. Mine felt just as real. Like Jacob, I refused to let go of God ... refused to give up the wrestling match until he blessed me. I was desperate for him to show me his comfort. I needed something tangible.

I heard someone recently say, "There is one thing to be said about wrestling with God. The alternative is to turn and run from him." That statement resonated with me. Part of me wanted to run. But I did not. I wrestled. I didn't know where else to go. To throw away my faith meant no possibility of hope at all.

My wrestling match with God went on for months. I'll tell you more about that later. But God did begin to bless me with kisses from heaven. It took a long time for the cumulative effect of these to wear me down. But as I held onto him, he also held onto me, refusing to release his grip. Finally, his love prevailed, bringing me to a place of surrender. Read onward and I will tell you the stories of his comfort and mercy.

A Poem – Found By Him
Frank Curtiss, February 2009

A promised land lays
  just over the river
A land overflowing
I can see its vineyards
  branches barely-able
  to bear its fruit
I smell the blossoms
  almond trees in bloom
I remember the taste
  of its fruit
Sweet-sticky nectar
  dripping down my beard
As a blind man
  longs to see
  the faces he has touched
So I long to cross the river
  again …
Oh yes, you see
  I have been there
  sent as a spy once
I still dream
  of the sweet water
  springing forth
  from underground rivers
Wild flowers
  ablaze upon
  the green rolling hills

fed by spring rains
And yet,
  like a nomad
  I wander this desert
By day I am scorched
My skin turns to leather
By night,
  my bones are made brittle
  by the chilling cold
And I dream,
My night dreams
  more vivid,
  than those of the day
It is at night
  I see the giants
I flee from them in terror
  lest they devour me
But there were two men
Two spies who crossed
  the river with me
  two who saw differently
Fear came to them also
Yet they acted courageously
  in the face of danger
For they knew
  in their heart
  that God was greater
Greater than all the giants
  of the land
Has my destiny been sealed?

Am I banished to wander
  this place of desolation
  all of my days?
My body food for vultures?
Praise be to God
  It shall not be so!
For he has written
  a new ending to the story
My sin of disbelief
  is forgiven
My days
  of worshipping
  the golden calf
  have been forgotten
And now,
  as I cross the river
  to that good land
Once again
  I feel that stony fear
But then,
  courage wells up inside of me!
I raise my eyes and see
  my mighty prince before me
His brilliance which emanates
  glints upon the armor
  of the warriors
  in whose midst I travel
And my heart is lifted!
Strength fills my bones
Joy overruns me

For his Spirit,
  the Spirit of Yeshua
  goes before me to battle
The giants shall be vanquished
And I shall reside
  forever with him
In the land of promise!

Chapter Seven:
Binding Up Our Broken Hearts

"God is close to the brokenhearted and saves those who are crushed in spirit."
Psalm 33:18 (NIV).

It is time to tell you about the first of many things God did, after Jenna's loss, to begin the process of binding our broken hearts. It happened in early April, just days after Jenna's death. It had been a rainy day. Then, as the afternoon sun sank low in the western sky, it dipped below the clouds and lit up the woods behind our home in brilliant light. I had a feeling there might be a rainbow, so I hurried out front to the street and looked back toward our house. It took my breath away, a vibrant rainbow which formed a perfect arc over our house from one horizon to the other.

I grabbed Teddy and Rhonda. I lifted a barefoot Teddy to keep her feet dry. As I did so, a thought came into my mind—seemingly from nowhere. I told her, "Look, Jesus sent you a rainbow. Your mommy asked him if he would send it to you from her. Jesus smiled as he said 'Of course.' Now, there it is." It was the first joy I had experienced since the day we'd learned of Jenna's death.

In that moment I believed what I told Teddy. But over time doubts crept in. I asked God for more rainbows, but none came, not yet anyway. But there is much more to this story. Some I'll share now, some later.

Rhonda and I love music. It has the power to bring joy, evoke peace, and can even help you grieve. We had a playlist we put together for that purpose. Some of the songs came from Jenna's own playlist, including a country song called "If I Die Young" by a group called The Band Perry. It seemed fitting. The song starts out with the lyrics from the title … *If I die young.*

I attempted to get permission to quote the exact lyrics but never received a response. So in my own words, a few lines later, she asks the Lord to make her a rainbow to shine down upon her grieving mother. She wants her to know that she is safe in the loving arms of God.

One day those lyrics caught my attention. I had listened to the song dozens of times but somehow had never heard those particular words. That evening, I played the song with Rhonda. She had never noticed these lyrics either. It gave her encouragement.

A few days later, we were in our car with Teddy, heading east to a restaurant for dinner. And reminiscent of that first rainbow, the setting sun put on quite a show in front of us, a brilliant rainbow set against a backdrop of billowing, dark-purple clouds. On one end, it was a double rainbow. Coincidence? Maybe. But for a time, our hearts were lifted up by this beautiful gift from God.

A Psalm: Who is this One that We Call God?
By Frank Curtiss, March 12, 2010

Our minds, though intricately woven by him,
    cannot grasp all that he is
For everything that we have seen and touched,
    has a beginning and an end
But God is not finite
He was never born
    nor created in some cosmic explosion
He has always been
    and yet not old
    at least not as we know age

He does not decay
   his bones do not creak
Yet he has more knowledge, greater wisdom,
    than all the history of men …
    all seers, all teachers, all kings
To what can we compare him?
Can we even catch a glimpse,
   of who he is and what he is about?
With feeble words I will try
   hoping to enlarge our idea of him
But this I know for certain,
   that every image I craft,
   every simile, each metaphor
   will fall laughably short,
   a child's bucket of sand
   upon the beaches of paradise
   a few bricks in a great cathedral
Do you see my folly?
Comparing God to what can be numbered?
God is a Master Artist
   his canvas … the universe
   and a baby in Mommy's womb
One is vast
One is small
   yet no less intricate
With a flourish of his brush
   he creates a great leviathan
   to swim the depths of the ocean
   to awe us as it leaps above the foam
With a dab of paint from his palette

a delicate pink seashell upon the sand
No two things are alike
   not a mighty mountain
   nor even a snowflake
   though we could never count them all
His creativity is effortless
He lies in rest upon a grassy knoll
   gazing skyward … watching in delight
   as his masterpiece unfolds before him
   for he set it all in motion long ago
God is an Author
Not one of fiction
   though he loves a good parable
No, he writes of the past …
   and of the present, which was once future
   and the future, which shall be present
These are all the same to him …
   the history of this earth
    just a speck of dust in time
Then he tells of a new heaven
   and a new earth to come
Men are his fingertips
   with which he holds his pen
He breathes his story into them
   a chapter here … a verse there
Many recorded in a single book
   countless more written in heaven
You are part of his story
   and so am I (one of the best parts!)
Stories of cowardice and noble deeds …

of simple men doing great things
   and mighty men who act as fools;
Stories of tragedy and despair ...
   hope, courage and faith
Does the story have a happy ending?
Yes ... though not really an ending
   for our days of joy and laughter
   shall never see an end
God is a Gardener
   not just in a figurative sense
He tends to great forests
   a place of shelter for many ...
   and in rocky, arid places
He coaxes a single cacti from the rock
   Thorny ... we have that in common
   a single pink flower forming its crown
Fly over the mountain ...
   and you will find a meadow
   riotously carpeted with wildflowers
Once he made a garden
   so lush, so beautiful, so tranquil ...
   we remember it as paradise
Our souls yearns for it still
Someday we shall return
   and walk its cool paths with our Father
   the same one who planted his son
   and called him a vine
With great skill he cut him
   so he could graft us in
His roots go deep ...

through inhospitable soil
to find the water table
 the source of life
so that our vine might be green
during the days of drought
Carefully the father tends to us …
 pruning us … training our vines …
 that we might bear clusters of his love
God is a Mighty King …
 King of Peace … King of Righteousness
Master of the domain he created
Yet he is no tyrant
He places no whip upon our back
Rather he left his throne in heaven …
 to live in our midst …
 serving us with two hands
He chose a lowly position …
 nine months in the dark womb
 of a poor young peasant girl
Reared not in king's palaces
 but in the weariest of villages
His hands, those hands of God …
 calloused from hard labor,
 reached out to the untouchable leper
 and made mud packs
 for the eyes of a blind beggar
He rode no royal carriage
His two feet carried him everywhere
 even upon stormy waters
And on his back, with flesh torn off

he carried a criminals cross
   dripping a path of tears and blood
   a trail for us to follow
Any man who believes God to be cruel
   has never considered these things
Is there an end to the things
   I could say about God?
No, the comparisons are as endless
   as God himself ...
The words I have penned
   a molecule of salt in the ocean
God is a sculptor, a potter, an architect ...
   our teacher, a travelling preacher ...
   the healer, and great physician ...
   he who makes us whole ...
He is a man acquainted with grief ...
   an anchor in the storm ...
   a hidden treasure ...
   an untamed Lion ...
   who roams wild and free
He is a sheep ...
   as well as the shepherd ...
A man and a Spirit ...
A Father and a son ...
The bridegroom ...
My lover ...
My brother ...
My friend

Chapter Eight:
Visions from God?

"I will go to the mountaintop with you—the mountain of suffering love."
Song of Songs 4:6 (TPT).

I had a powerful experience a few months after losing Jenna. I hesitate to call it a vision. I don't know what to call it except a powerful mental image, so strong that it is burned into my memory as if it actually took place.

I was working in my home office and listening to music. A song came on by a Christian artist named David Crowder. I'm not a huge fan of most contemporary Christian music, but David Crowder is an exception. His music feels real to me ... close to the surface. The song is called "Oh Great God Give Us Rest." A portion of the lyrics are as follows:

> *Oh great God give us rest*
> *We're all worn thin from all of this*
> *At the end of our hope with nothing left*
> *Oh great God give us rest*

As I listened to the lyrics, I suddenly saw an image of myself, standing before Jesus, like a child standing before his father. As I stood there with my feet planted, I was beating on his chest with both fists, screaming and sobbing, "Why...why...why?"

Jesus did not appear to be taken aback or offended by my attack. He stood firmly, gazing at me with tender, knowing eyes.

He did not say a thing, did not try to answer my question. I've always had a sense that he knew there was nothing he could say, no answer he could give me at that moment that would satisfy my soul.

I've often thought about this experience, wondering if it was from God. If it was, it showed me that he understood the sadness and pain in my heart and was willing to let me pour it all out on him. He is big enough to take it all—all of my sorrows, all of my grief—and to respond with patience and great compassion. Whether or not this was from him, this is the God I long to believe in.

*****

A month or two later, I had an experience that bore similarities. Music again played a part in my grieving experience. For me, music has a way of bringing my deepest emotions to the surface. You might wonder if that is a good thing. I found it to be a necessary part of my healing.

This time, the experience occurred in a worship service on a Sunday morning. I was standing in the back of the auditorium, doing my greeting duties, when our youth pastor gave an invitation to those who were struggling with faith and trust. I stepped forward. A compassionate friend put his hands on my shoulder and prayed for me. I felt nothing at that moment except the love of a friend.

I went and took my seat next to Rhonda. Our worship team began to play a song, "You Won't Relent." This song, by Misty Edwards, has always brought my heart to a place of worship. On this occasion, it washed over me like a tidal wave, pulling me out to sea in its undertow. I lifted my hands toward heaven. Before I knew it, I was on my knees, tears streaming down my face.

There is a reference in that song to God being a seal upon my heart, and upon my arm. It goes on to say that there is a love as strong as death. If you're not familiar with the song, I highly recommend that you listen to it.

As the words were sung, I thought of the crown of thorns, tattooed as a seal upon my arm. This thought comes to me every time I hear this song.

Suddenly, another image filled my mind's eye. I was staring into the face of Jesus as he hung upon the cross. His tormented face occupied my vision ... disfigured, bruised, swollen, bloodied. The thorns of that crown were imbedded in his brow. In his bloodshot eyes I could see all of the world's sin, pain, and sorrow.

I stared, riveted by this image. He raised his vision and locked eyes with mine. I felt naked before him. Then, a single tear ran down his cheek. I knew that tear was for me. He did not speak, but the following words entered my mind, *"Today your children are with me in paradise."* I knew it was because of the great price he was paying ... more than enough to cover their many sins; and mine.

I was undone. All I could do was cry; my tears a strange mixture of sorrow and deep gratitude for the price he was paying (I use present tense, because that is how it felt).

*****

That night, as I pondered this, the words written by a prophet named Isaiah came to mind. I found them in his book:

"See, my servant will act wisely;
he will be raised and lifted up and highly exalted.

Just as there were many who were appalled at him—
his appearance was so disfigured beyond that of any human being
and his form marred beyond human likeness—"

Isaiah 52:13,14 (NIV).

"Surely, he took up our pain and bore our suffering,
yet we considered him punished by God,
stricken by him, and afflicted.

But he was pierced for our transgressions,
he was crushed for our iniquities;
the punishment that brought us peace was on him,
and by his wounds we are healed."
Isaiah 53:4,5 (NIV).

What does this vision mean to me? It is my habit to question the legitimacy of my experience. Yet here I am, more than ten years later, and this image comes to mind often, especially in times of doubt. Whether a genuine vision, or something my mind conjured up, matters little to me. Either way, I am undone to the core by the love and mercy of the one who hung on that cross, that my children might be bought by his blood, and that I might be healed of this great sorrow.

Here is one of my earliest psalms:

Psalm: You are an Awesome God

Frank Curtiss, January 2002

Lord, you are an awesome God
Your mercies, rich and bountiful
You reach down your hand to me
You lift me from the depths of despair
When my heart had no hope
You chose to meet me in that place
What more could I hope and desire
Than to live in your presence, Lord
My trials have been many
The pain has weighed me down
At night, my heart cries out to you
But in the morning you bring me joy

You never promised me an easy road
Only that you would bring me rest
My greatest desire is to be
A man after your own heart, Jesus
To that noble end O Lord
I know I must face many trials
My path will traverse many valleys
I will stand in awe upon many hilltops
But I know without a doubt
in the deepest, darkest valley,
    I will find you there
You will escort me
    through every trial and travail
And set my feet again on higher ground

Chapter Nine: God's Compassion in the Hearts of Men

"When I look at the night sky and see the work of your fingers—the moon and the stars that you set in place—what are mere mortals that you should think about them, human beings that you should care for them?"
Psalm 8:3,4 (NIV).

Though God had begun to show himself to me through signs in the heavens (rainbows), and images of himself that gave me comfort, so much more was needed. As the weeks and months go by, the world moves on, but you feel like you never will. I was still in need of more tangible touches of God—more kisses from his Holy Spirit.

I have often described sorrow using the metaphor of waves. I grew up in Huntington Beach, California, so I love the ocean. A beach on a sunny morning with the sun burning away the mist is my happy place. A cool breeze in my face, the smell of sea air, the sand between my toes, waves washing over my feet. I feel God's smile.

I spent my summers at the beach. I never learned to surf, something I regret. I grew up body surfing and boogie boarding. I understand a great deal about the ocean and the action of waves. Mostly, that they can be unpredictable. You walk along the shore, thinking you know the boundary of the waves, then suddenly, a big one comes along, nearly knocking you off your feet. If it's a really big one, it might suck you out to sea as it retreats.

73

Grieving is like that. It comes in waves. Some small, some large, and some like a tsunami. And you never know what will trigger the big ones that nearly drown you. I still have these waves come over me at the most unexpected times.

Throughout our grieving nearly all of our family and friends were amazingly supportive, each in whatever way they understood. Not everyone knows how to act around a grieving person. Typically, those who have been through significant loss understand best how to be there for others. Usually just a hug and an ear are the best response. Sometimes people surprise you. That is the next part of my story, a story of three friends that surprised me.

*****

A prophetic psalm before I tell the story:

A Psalm: Walking the Hard Road Together
Frank Curtiss, June 18, 2002

I called out to God …
What do you say to me today?
What words of life do you speak?
This is what my heart heard …
This is God's Spirit
I dwell deep within you
In the innermost recess of your heart
Be quiet and I will speak
Be still and listen intently
My words are words of life
Let me show you the way to live
Trust me with your life
I will bring you no harm
Believe that it is my desire

To bless you with every good thing
Know that I am your God
I chose you from among all mankind
Know that you are my child
And that I have a purpose for you
Ask, and I shall give you wisdom
Seek, and I will give you courage
Obey, and I will find joy in you
Be still, and experience my love
You say you want contentment
It is yours, grab hold of it
You've asked me to give you joy
No need to ask, it is yours for the taking
Follow the path I have placed before you
It is well lit and easy to see
At times I will take you to hard places
Places you believe you do not want to go
There is a path which bypasses hardship, or so it seems
But if you choose that path, you go alone
My path may look impossible to traverse
But I will carry you on my shoulders
So let us walk the path together
Traverse the hard places side-by-side
Huge blessings await on the other side
Rewards you cannot fathom

The first friend I ran into was at a wedding—one of Jenna's friends—the summer after Jenna left us. I had not seen John for months. He asked how I was doing. When he locked eyes with me, I could see he wanted an honest answer. As I opened my heart to him ... just a crack ... tears began to run down his cheeks. I was caught off guard. Though I considered him a good friend, I had never seen him display this kind of emotion. I realized then that I had vastly underestimated his heart.

The second event occurred the very next morning as we were coming out of church. Another close friend named Phil, whom I had seen often since Jenna's death, asked me the same question ... *How are you doing?* As with John, I could sense the sincerity in his question. As I feebly tried to answer, he too began to cry. Once again, I found myself surprised. I knew he cared for me and my family like a brother, but he is a man who does not display his emotions easily.

As I pondered these two events, I began to sense that I was seeing God's heart for me, expressed through my friends. But in my doubt, I put a fleece before God, a test to see if this was really him. I asked him ... *If this is really of you, God, please cause this to happen a third time. You know I'm struggling. You know I have doubts. I need to know that you exist, and that you really care.*

Months went by ... nothing ... just another unanswered prayer. Then, one Sunday morning I was greeting people at church. An old friend came along whom I had not seen in nearly a year, since before we lost Jenna. He asked how I was doing. I asked if he had heard about our daughter. He had not.

As I told him about Jenna, he began to bawl like a baby. Later, in church, his tears flowed again. I had never seen this man cry before. We were casual friends, and he had always struck me as a happy-go-lucky guy ... easygoing, fun, playful, a big kid in many ways. But on this day, I saw a different side of him.

We had a time of sharing at church that morning. And I told this story, the story of three men who cried ... three men from whom I did not expect such emotions ... showing me the heart of God.

Chapter Ten:
A Double Portion

*"Instead of your shame you will receive a double portion,
and instead of disgrace you will rejoice in your inheritance.
And so you will inherit a double portion in your land,
and everlasting joy will be yours."*
Isaiah 61:7 (NIV).

About a year after losing Jenna, we took a vacation to visit Rhonda's sister and brother-in-law who had moved to a suburb of Charleston, and to take our granddaughter, Teddy, to Orlando. Rhonda's mother and father-in-law also came to South Carolina. It was a mini family reunion.

It was a warm spring day in Charleston as we sat in the shade of stately oaks on an historic plantation, listening to a woman sing and tell stories of her people. She was a descendant of the Gullah people ... the African American people who were ripped away from their homeland in West Africa and brought as slaves to the lowland areas of the South, primarily South Carolina and Georgia. I was transported to another time and place as she told of the hardships of her people ... stories of their sorrow, their courage, and their faith.

Her storytelling was masterful. She finished by repeating several times ... "This is the story of my people ... *my* story ... *your* story ... this is *our* story." Then, with seamless transition, she added ... "This is *his* story ... *his* story ... his-story ... history." The realization dawned on me. This really is *his* story. *Our* story is part of *his* story. It is our *history*.

77

*****

The evening prior, three of us had sat up past midnight telling our own stories. It was one of those conversations that can only take place among those who have experienced deep sorrow. My mother-in-law Marva, sister-in-law Ruby Kay, and I had outlasted the rest of the family that night. One by one, the others had wandered off to bed.

Allow me to give you a little backstory. Rhonda's sister, Ruby, lost her only son Jason to murder thirteen years previously. Her life has never been the same. She walked through hell. Sorrow changed her. But not for the worse. She is a woman of considerable compassion who loves to help others deal with their own pain. Though she lost her only child, she is a grandmother. Jason had a son, only a baby at the time of his death. I smiled when I heard Ruby describe how he was the spitting image of Jason, so much so that she sometimes forgets and calls him by that name. I could relate.

She told us a story about how some well-meaning person had given her a book, *When Bad Things Happen to Good People*. She said that when she finished the book, she threw it across the room in anger ... anger at God, rage against her son's killer, and anger at the world that refused to stop and grieve.

My mother-in-law, Marva, rarely speaks of her own losses. She tends to keep her sorrows bottled up, while presenting a cheerful exterior. But if you pay attention, you catch glimpses through the cracks in her armor, and little by little her story unfolds ... a story of ninety years. Marva was born into a very large family, eleven children, living a meager existence in the arid Southwest. Her father abandoned them after their mother had a stroke. Marva was raised by her older sisters. Years later, she lost Rhonda's dad to alcoholism and divorce (he later died of cancer). She later nursed another husband through the last years of his life.

On top of that, Ruby's loss of Jason, and our loss of Joel and Jenna, are Marva's losses too ... three grandchildren gone before their time. But possibly the hardest experience of all was the loss of her own son Steve, Ruby and Rhonda's little brother. Steve was caught in the flames of an apartment fire. He was so severely burned, head to toe, that the doctors gave him less than a one percent chance to survive. By some miracle, he lived more than a dozen years after that. But knowing of his suffering may have been even harder than if he had died in the fire.

Yet with all her losses, Marva has had one huge blessing in these latter years of her life ... her husband Virgil. Marva and Virgil had known each other for decades, but did not marry until late in life after both were widowed. They are true soul mates who have greatly enriched one another's lives. At the time of our trip, Virgil was having some health issues. I could see the worry on Marva's face. Thankfully, he recovered.

As the three of us sat up late, drinking wine and talking of life's joys and sorrows, I told them some of our story—*his-story*—of how God appeared to be reaching down to us. Little did I know it was only the beginning of this chapter. Let me go back even further and relate the backstory to you ...

*****

On a Sunday evening a few weeks prior to our trip, we were hosting our pastor, Lee, his wife Sue, and other friends for a church meeting. Lee had a tradition of asking each person to share how they were doing before we got down to business. When it came my turn, I laid it all on the table. I told them of my crisis of faith and my wrestling match with God. I related how I was looking for tangible signs from God and asked them to pray for me, and for us. It had been a hard winter. Rhonda had been struggling for weeks with colds and flu viruses. And I was plagued with hip pain (a whole other story in itself, thankfully no longer an issue).

In Lee's sermons, he had been speaking from Isaiah 61, focusing on the promise of verse 7 which I quoted at the beginning of the chapter:

"Instead of your shame you will receive a double portion,
and instead of disgrace you will rejoice in your inheritance.
And so you will inherit a double portion in your land,
and everlasting joy will be yours." Isaiah 61:7 (NIV).

He tied those to a verse from 2 Corinthians, to talk about it being a season of God's favor. In his letter to the Corinthian church, Paul had written:

"For he (God) says, 'In the time of my favor I heard you, and in the day of salvation I helped you.' I tell you, now is the time of God's favor, now is the day of salvation."

2 Corinthians 6:2 (NIV).

Like all people, we desired to see God's favor in our lives, to feel his blessing, to know his love. We desired to receive his everlasting joy—joy which goes beyond our circumstances—beyond our sorrow.

We had not been feeling it. Not even close. Rhonda's sickness, my hip, struggles with our business, all piled on top of our continued grieving over the loss of our two children. It felt like God and the world had turned against us.

Our friends gathered around us to pray. Some had encouraging words to speak over us. One friend spoke of God giving us "beauty for ashes" ... that beautiful image from Isaiah 61:3. But one word stood above all of the others. One of our pastors, Ray Moody, said that he was seeing an image of a double rainbow over us. He didn't understand what it meant, yet shared it anyway, thinking it spoke of a double portion of favor in our lives.

Goosebumps crawled up my arm. The image shot straight to my heart like an arrow. Ray had no idea of the symbolic meaning rainbows had taken on in our lives. After the meeting, I told him the story, explaining why the image of the double rainbow meant much more to me than God's favor. For me, the two arcs of that rainbow were a representation of God's covering over our two children. I believed God was again showing us once again that our children were under his covering ... joyfully living in his Kingdom.

Ray said that because he did not understand the image God was showing him, he almost put a lid on it. I was so glad he chose not to. The rest of this story would have far less significance if he had not taken the risk to share what God had given him.

*****

Five days later, I was working my Friday night shift at our restaurant. It had been a rainy afternoon. In the middle of the busy dinner rush, I looked outside and saw the evening sun shining brightly, reflecting off the raindrops which were still falling. I knew it was the perfect condition for a rainbow.

I had customers to look after, but I was not to be deterred. I stepped outside. There it was—just as I had expected—a beautiful rainbow. It was not very bright at first, but as the sun continued to drop toward the horizon it got brighter and brighter. I was crazy busy, but kept looking outside anyway, and then I saw what my soul desired most ... the seven brilliant colors of a double rainbow!

My heart couldn't help but feel a sense of wonder. I knew God was reassuring me again ... that he was real ... that he cared ... that our children were okay with him. Their love, and his, was shining down on us.

I shared this story with Marva and Ruby Kay on that late evening. I could see that they, too, found comfort in it. But wait, there's more to the story. But first a psalm:

A Psalm: Who Can Know the Ways of God?

Frank Curtiss, December 13, 2002

Who Can Know the Ways of God?
Who can measure his mercies?

Can a man grasp the depth of his affection?
His grace shown in such abundance?
I long to truly know it
To fathom the riches of this love
Can my heart fully comprehend it?
Can my mind encircle it?
I am incapable of it Yeshua
But your Spirit can teach it to me
Your Spirit knows the mysteries
He is able to enlarge my understanding
But is my heart ready for such knowledge?
Will it be overwhelmed?
It seems my heart would burst …
   should I learn a tenth of it
I say I want to be a man …
   who has the heart of God
I know my purpose is to love
   my fellow man with your love
If I am able, Lord, God …
   it will only be by your power
My soul is not able to love as you do
When I try on my own I always fail
Enable me, Lord … empower me
Mold my heart like clay
Create a vessel for your glory
Overpower my flesh with your love
My old man will fight you
His death is slow and painful
But die he must … so I can live
To experience all you have for me

Chapter Eleven:
Signs in the Heavens

"All that he does in us is designed to make us a mature church for his pleasure, until we become a source of praise to him—glorious and radiant, beautiful and holy, without fault or flaw."
Ephesians 5:27 (TPT).

Journal Entry: A Prayer
Frank Curtiss, August 8, 2005

May the wisdom of God
Come down to me
May the blessing of God
Rest Upon me
May the heart of God
Become my heart
May the face of God
Shine upon me
May the joy of God
Become my joy
May I trust in God
All the days of my life
May I love God
With all of my heart and soul
And may I always
Dwell in his presence

After four wonderful days in Charleston, Rhonda, Teddy, and I made the long drive south to Orlando for the second half of our vacation. On the first day, we took Teddy to *The Wizarding World of Harry Potter*. We had scattered showers throughout the day, which continued overnight. The next morning, I stepped outside to see if the weather was clearing as was forecast. What I came upon took my breath away. There in the morning sky hung a strikingly beautiful double rainbow. I hurried to bring Rhonda and Teddy outside. The moment Rhonda was coming out the door, she received a text from her sister Ruby, "OMG, they're showing a double rainbow in Orlando on the news! Have you seen it?" The knowledge that Ruby Kay was sharing this extraordinary gift with us made it even more special.

*****

We spent four fun-packed days in Orlando, enjoying Disneyworld and Epcot, then headed home to Seattle—back to the real world. I came home to a project, the possible relocation of our restaurant. Our landlords were planning to sell our building to a developer. We had been doing business there for over twenty years. We had found another spot and were in negotiations with an overworked property manager.

A few days after we returned, I finally had the opportunity to meet him face to face, along with two of his associates. The meeting went well, but that's not why I'm telling you this story. We were sitting at a table near the window. Suddenly, one of them looked up and said, "O wow, look, there's a rainbow." In that moment, the business meeting became secondary. I excused myself and stepped outside. Yes, you guessed it—I was greeted by another brilliant double rainbow. I was moved to tears, so much so that I told my story to these people whom I barely knew.

A beautiful part of this story is that Rhonda and Teddy also saw the rainbows which I had seen from the restaurant. It was clear that God wanted to touch Ruby Kay's heart as well. The next morning, I got a text from her at four in the morning. She had seen our third double rainbow on *Good Morning America*. I knew she could sense it too. God was revealing his heart to us all. To top it off, that morning there was a picture of that rainbow on the front page of the *Seattle Times*. It was that glorious.

*****

I have told this story to many people in the years since. I'm surprised how many people tell me that they've never seen a double rainbow. I don't recall ever seeing one as a full arc prior to these.

What does a man make of such a phenomenon? Within weeks of Ray's vision, we saw three glorious double rainbows. I could have been a cynic, called it a coincidence, but it seemed way beyond that. I took it as touches from a loving, merciful God. Ten years later, I am still in awe.

When we saw the rainbow a couple of days after Jenna's death, it was comforting. It felt like a sign from God ... a sign of his love. I wanted it to be. But I had my doubts. Then there was the song, "If I Die Young," and the rainbow we experienced a few days later. That, too, felt like God. But my mind still questioned it.

But after these three double rainbows, I no longer believed I could question God's gift. It was an unmistakable sign of his great love for us ... and that my children are living under the shadow of his wing.

Do you recall that I was hoping for some sign from God? One day I had written in my journal ... "I have concluded that the greatest desire of my heart is to have full, unshakeable confidence that my children are with God and that one day we will all be reunited again." Later, I went on to write ... "I had hoped for some big, life-changing event to share, or some great revelation. I like my stories to be neatly wrapped between a good beginning and a meaningful ending." And yet I had concluded that I would probably not receive one, stating "Stories about life are not always like that."

I am still living in amazement that my conclusion was wrong. God proved himself trustworthy. He has shown me his unmistakable love in a way I cannot deny. He found a way to comfort my heart ... a way I never would have imagined.

Losing my children was painful beyond words. I miss them every day. But now I live in full confidence. One day, we will be reunited. We will live together forever in God's Kingdom. In light of eternity, this brief time of pain will fade away. With that hope, I can now walk freely in joy.

Chapter Twelve: Words of Comfort from an Ancient Prophet

My favorite book in the Bible is the book of Isaiah, often referred to as the fifth gospel. During the days of my deepest sorrow, it ministered to me in ways I cannot express. In chapter 53, Isaiah prophesies of the suffering that Jesus would go through. Listen to the words he penned:

> *"He was despised and rejected—a man of sorrows, acquainted with the deepest grief.*
>
> *We turned our backs on him and looked the other way. He was despised, and we did not care.*
>
> *Yet it was our weaknesses he carried; it was our sorrows that weighed him down.*
>
> *And we thought his troubles were a punishment from God, a punishment for his own sins!*
>
> *But he was pierced for our rebellion, crushed for our sins.*
>
> *He was beaten so we could be whole. He was whipped so we could be healed.*
>
> *All of us, like sheep, have strayed away. We have left God's paths to follow our own.*
>
> *Yet the LORD laid on him the sins of us all."*
>
> Isaiah 53:3-6 (NLT).

Jesus understood sorrow firsthand. Notice that he is called *"a man of sorrows, acquainted with deepest grief."* If we read carefully, I believe we will identify two reasons for his sorrow.

First, that he was *"despised and rejected."* God the Son, our creator, left his place in heaven to come down to earth to show us the Kingdom of God, to show us how to live. He came to live as one of us, then to suffer and die for us, yet we turned our back on him and sent him to the most horrible death.

The second reason—an even greater sorrow, I believe—was that all of our sorrow was placed upon him … *"it was our sorrows that weighed him down."* Can you imagine the weight of all the world's sorrow upon you? Every loss—yours, mine—the sorrows of all of mankind—every sin, every regret. It is no wonder his death came about more quickly than expected.

There is another sorrow hinted at here which is brought to light in the gospels when Jesus hung on the cross. Matthew 27:46 records Jesus' words, *"My God, my God, why have you abandoned me?"* (NIV). Other translations use the word *"forsaken."* These exact words had been written in Psalm 22, a Psalm written by David centuries before, which provided a graphic prophecy of Jesus' suffering.

There is a commonly held teaching that God was unable to look upon Jesus, as the great weight of our sins was upon him. I believe it may have been that the immense guilt of that sin, and all of our sorrow, caused Jesus to *feel* separated from the Father. The latter makes more sense to me because of a verse which shows up later in Psalm 22, *"For he (God) has not despised or scorned the suffering of the afflicted one; he has not hidden his face from him but has listened to his cry for help."* Psalm 22:24 (NIV).

Either way, he who had always had the closest possible relationship with the Father, now felt his absence. I can only imagine what that moment must have been like. Yet it is because he experienced that pain that he can be such comfort to us in our sorrows—in those times when we, too, feel that God has turned his back on us.

*****

Are you familiar with the story of when Jesus walked into the synagogue in Nazareth and read from the scroll of the prophet Isaiah? Afterward, he looked around and said to them, *"Today this scripture is fulfilled in your hearing."* Luke 4:18-21 (NIV).

The place that he read from was Isaiah 61, verse one and the first part of verse two (of course, there were no verse numbers on the scrolls). The Jews were well acquainted with this prophecy. They knew it spoke of the coming Messiah. Because of that understanding, it created a near-riot and they tried to throw Jesus off a cliff. He did not fit their bill. They were looking for a mighty king.

The reason I mention these verses is because the first three verses of Isaiah 61 became a lifeline to me. When I was at a point of disbelief—of feeling abandoned by the Father—these words somehow managed to find their way through the stone wall I had erected around my heart.

"The Spirit of the Sovereign LORD is on me, because the LORD has anointed me to proclaim good news to the poor. He has sent me to bind up the brokenhearted, to proclaim freedom for the captives and release from darkness for the prisoners, to proclaim the year of the LORD's favor and the day of vengeance of our God, to comfort all who mourn, and provide for those who grieve in Zion— to bestow on them a crown of beauty instead of ashes, the oil of joy instead of mourning, and a garment of praise instead of a spirit of despair. They will be called oaks of righteousness, a planting of the LORD for the display of his splendor."
Isaiah 61:1-3 (NIV).

I have underlined those parts which told me that—despite all he had allowed me to suffer—Jesus could be trusted with my heart.

I declare to you now that Jesus has accomplished all of these things in our hearts. It was more than the miraculous signs that he showed us. It was a work of his Holy Spirit. He has bound up our broken hearts. He released us from darkness. He has comforted us. He has bestowed a crown of beauty upon our head—something only he could do. He has given us a garment of praise instead of a spirit of despair.

A Psalm: Renewed In Your Presence
Frank Curtiss, May 2, 2007

Your word, O Lord, instructs me
It invites me into your presence
There, in the presence of your holiness
I am renewed
You give me a clean heart
A desire to seek after you
Your Holy Spirit comes
It rests upon me
I am comforted
In your presence I find peace
Joy begins to come alive
In supplication and praise
   trust reawakens
I find new strength
You, O Lord are the God
   of all the universe
All of nature bows to your whim
Who am I that you consider me
   worthy of adoption?

Chapter Thirteen: From Mourning to Rejoicing

"You have turned my wailing into dancing; you removed my sackcloth and clothed me with joy, that my heart may sing your praises and not be silent. Lord my God, I will praise you forever." Psalm 30:11,12 (NIV).

God's purpose is restoration. God always desires to make right what is wrong in our lives so we can live joyfully and abundantly. There are many, many verses regarding how he restores us, pours out his favor, and fills us with his joy. I honestly didn't think it was possible after all we'd been through.

Our pastor, Todd Puckett, recently said something that struck home, *"The deeper the mourning, the deeper the comfort. Enter into mourning until his faith is released in you."* It rang true because it is exactly what we have experienced. He accomplished the impossible, exchanging the ashes of our sorrow for his joy.

A Psalm: Welcome Home
By Frank Curtiss, September 25, 2006

You have been my God
From the days of my youth
You called me as a lad
And drew my heart to you
I followed you for a time
By instinct I loved you

91

My spirit knew you
But I also loved sin
The desires of my flesh
  overwhelmed me
So I turned away from you
I trampled underfoot
The gifts you had given me
But you O Lord, Jesus
Were merciful to forgive
You continued to call my heart
You showed me the wages of my sin
You made my heart restless
  for you once again
Slowly I returned
Crawling upon my knees
For I could not stand
But you lifted my face
You took my hand
And lifted me to my feet
You restored my place at the family table
To the seat which had sat vacant
While I ran away from you
You smiled warmly and said,
"Welcome home my child"

Here are a few of my favorite promises, all of which now speak of my own experience:

"Those who sow with tears will reap with songs of joy. Those who go out weeping, carrying seed to sow, will return with songs of joy, carrying sheaves with them." *Psalm 126:5,6 (NIV).*

Jeremiah speaks a similar promise:

> *"They will come and shout for joy on the heights of Zion; they will rejoice in the bounty of the Lord—The grain, the new wine and the olive oil, the young of the flocks and herds. They will be like a well-watered garden, and they will sorrow no more. Then the young women will dance and be glad, young men and old as well. I will turn their mourning into gladness; I will give them comfort and joy instead of sorrow." Jeremiah 31:12,13 (NIV).*

I love that Jeremiah mentions *old men* here. I'm getting there, though thankfully Rhonda and I have been blessed with good health. I took a twenty-five-mile bike ride this morning with a young woman who is like a daughter to me. She's a serious rider, not even half my age, and I almost kept up!

Notice all of the agricultural references in these verses. These would have been very relatable to people in the days when these were being written. There were no grocery stores, no corporate farms feeding tens of thousands. Most people grew their own food and raised their own animals, or they traded their services with those that did. I can relate well to these references because I am a gardener and a chef. These things speak to me. I love that he says that we, *"will be like a well-watered garden."* I picture a lush, abundant garden, producing more than I can possibly eat. It must be shared.

There is one more verse which I feel helps us understand all of this. No one likes to go through loss. Yet God uses our experiences to help others:

> *"Praise be to the God and Father of our Lord Jesus Christ, the Father of compassion and the God of all comfort, who comforts us in all our troubles, so that we can comfort those in any trouble with the comfort we ourselves receive from God. For just as we share abundantly in the sufferings of Christ, so also our comfort abounds through Christ." 2 Corinthians 1:3-5 (NIV).*

Does that mean God punishes us with pain so that we can comfort others? No. God is only good. He does not inflict pain. But he will not allow our experiences to be wasted. He will use the pain in our lives to bring refining in our own lives. He will also use it to mature us so that we can help others in their times of pain.

I believe that most of the pain we experience in this life is the result of living in a broken world. Quite often it is even the result, the natural consequences, of our own poor choices. We ought not to confuse this and consider it punishment from God.

I know I've quoted a lot of verses in this chapter but I am going to leave you with two more:

"When you speak healing words, you offer others fruit from the tree of life." Proverbs 15:4 (TPT).

"Nothing is more appealing than speaking beautiful, life-giving words. For they release sweetness to our souls and inner healing to our spirits." Proverbs 16:24 (TPT).

One more poem by my own hand to lay a foundation for the next chapter:

A Poem – Broken Shackles
By Frank Curtiss, December 22, 2010

I have tried and tried

My fingers are raw, bloodied

From digging, digging

Moving stone … bones of trees

Things long dead, lodged within the earth

Searching, seeking … for that buried place

The deepest part of my soul

It cries out to me to be free

Is it I who imprisoned it?
Placed chains upon it?
Locked it away …
In some dank, dreary dungeon?
Not far from where hell exists?
Without illumination … it lies beneath the walls …
    of the castle I have built … built around my heart
Without illumination … seemingly unsearchable
If I found it … would the lamp I carry …
    reach its darkest corners,
    where my deepest feelings hide?
The ones which overpower me
I have a ring of keys, collected from men
They tell me they can unlock the chains
Rumors circle about that some have unbound
    the lock which binds their hands
But have any found the key …
    to the shackles upon their feet?
The ones that keep them …
    from running free?
Free upon the soft hills bathed in sunlight?
I see visions in my mind
Most men do not even search
Do they believe it is hopeless?
Do they even know that they have a soul?
Other men search
But only outside of themselves
They stare at a box
    which emits light and sound
But no life is found there

Though all of man's wisdom
  has been poured into it
What hope do they have …
  of ever finding the spring …
  from which their life flows?
So why do I search …
  like a man crazed with thirst?
If I found that place …
Could I change …
  the man I have become?
Could I slay the dragons …
  that infringe upon my sanity?
Could I tame the passions …
The selfish desires …
Which make war against …
  the man I desire to be?
Would I be free?
Unbeknownst to me, a man arrives
He has been watching
He sits down beside me
My body heaves in exhaustion
The clothes upon my back, tattered
I am nearly drowned In pools of sweat
Mingled with tears and blood
His look puzzles me
No worry creases his brow
But as our eyes lock,
I feel his compassion …
  it pours forth like healing balm
Like that of a mother …

comforting her injured child
Why does he seem happy …
   as he looks on my condition?
He utters no words
But I hear him all the same
As though our two hearts …
Speak to one another
I try to silence the voices …
   of desperation in my head
So I can hear him
His words always come quietly
"Come, follow me," he says
"I cannot," I protest …
   "My feet are shackled"
"Look again," he says to me
My eyes follow his gaze …
   downward to my feet
He laughs at my astonishment
As I see the broken shackles
Lying upon the cold stone
He rises to go
"Wait," I protest, "Where are you going?"
   suddenly, afraid to leave this dark place
"To walk upon the hills. The sun is warm."
"Aren't you coming?"
As we rise to go … ascending from the dungeon
   the last thing I see is the guard,
Now shackled in the chains I wore
And then we emerge into the light

Chapter Fourteen: It's All About Hope

"The righteous cried out, and Adonai heard, and he saved them from all their troubles. Adonai is near those with broken hearts; he saves those whose spirit is crushed." Psalm 34:18,19 (CJB).

I threw you a curve ball here by quoting from the *Complete Jewish Bible*. Few people I know are familiar with this translation. I was introduced to it by a friend a couple of years ago. In other translations, this is verses 17 and18. In the Psalms, the CJB begins with the first verse being the introduction to the Psalm, which is not numbered in other translations.

God is a seeker. He leaves the ninety-nine to find the one lost sheep. He sent his Son to seek the lost and broken, to save those whose spirit is crushed. One of the reasons any of us get lost is that we lose hope. Jesus understands the importance of hope. When mine was dashed, hanging by a thread, he came to me. And he came to my wife Rhonda.

Listen to these words written during this time of transition:

A Psalm – An Unwelcome Friend

By Frank Curtiss, September 21, 2009

Discouragement comes to visit me
an unwelcome friend
one who is banned from my table
because he has betrayed me.

He wears me down
  with his useless banter.
Setting me in a foul mood.
I become angry with those I should not.
Praise runs away from my lips.
Thankfulness crouches in a dark corner.
Gratitude refuses a seat at the table
  unwilling to raise a glass
  with he who prophecies gloom.
O why did I invite him in?
I feel a soft knock at the door.
My unwelcome guest becomes agitated.
Gripping my arm tightly
  he bids me not to answer.
I catch a glint of fear in his eyes
  as warm light penetrates
  the cracks in the door.
Had I sent out another invitation?
Nonetheless, this new arrival intrigues me.
  I whisper aloud
  "Come in my forgotten friend."
"I have another visitor."
"Come and sit at my table with us."
As the door slowly opens
  light invades the dark spaces.
Discouragement, who despises the light
  attempts to drag me away.
It is hard to pry away his fingers
  as he flees through the back door
  unable to withstand the illumination
  which washes over the room of my weary soul.

At my lowest moments I had seriously considered throwing in the towel on my faith. We had prayed and prayed for our children. Now, I felt God had ignored the deep cries of my heart. I still do not understand why he allowed my children to take their lives. I don't believe I will until I get to the promised land. Maybe not even then. But when I arrive there, and we are reunited, I doubt it will even matter to me.

It is hard to have faith in God when your trust has been shattered and hope lost. Hope is built on faith and trust—on believing what God says is true. When those things are shattered, hope is too.

Rhonda and I could have chosen to turn away from God. We also could have chosen to walk away from one another. Few marriages survive such losses. When parents lose children to suicide, the divorce rate soars to over seventy percent. I observed first-hand the reasons for this when I was involved in a suicide support group. Every person in the group was crushed by the suicide of someone they loved. Many blamed themselves—and many were facing blame from spouses or other family members.

But God refused to let go of us. Little by little, piece by piece, by the miraculous signs he gave us—along with the work of his Holy Spirit and the Word—he began to rebuild and restore our trust and renew our hope.

I mentioned earlier in the book my own reason for choosing to hold on to God. Although my hope was shattered, I realized that without him there was no hope at all. In Proverbs, Solomon wrote, *"Hope deferred makes the heart sick."* I truly don't know how anyone can survive in this world without it. And aside from God, our hope is for this life only.

God exchanges our mourning for his joy. Our mourning is an invitation for the comforter. God himself draws near. The Greek word used in the Bible for comforter is *parakletos,* which means "someone who is called to come alongside." In the New

Testament it is used to refer to the Holy Spirit and is also translated advocate, counselor, or helper.

Another thing that God does to give us hope is he gives us promises. He often reveals them to us when we need them most. We can help ourselves out tremendously by spending time in his Word, for that is how most of them are revealed to us.

When I needed it most, God reminded me of a promise he had given to us before either of our children took their lives, during the days when our world felt broken because of their choices and rebellion. It had already meant a great deal to me prior to our losses. Now I clung to it for dear life. The promise first came to me one morning when I was reading his Word, once again from the book of Isaiah (can you see why it is my favorite book?). It can be found in chapter 60, one chapter before the great consolations of chapter 61.

> *"Lift up your eyes and look about you: All assemble and come to you; your sons come from afar, and your daughters are carried on the hip. Then you will look and be radiant, and your heart will throb and swell with joy."* Isaiah 60:4-5 (NIV).

I remember the day this verse leapt off the page at me. I knew it was a promise God was giving to Rhonda and me to help us trust. For me it was a *rhema* word of the Lord … a living word. It contains some of the most beautiful imagery I have ever read, *"… your sons come from afar, and your daughters are carried on the hip (or arm). Then you will look and be radiant, your heart will throb and swell with joy."* I can feel the joy of it even now.

The context of this verse is the return of God's children to the New Jerusalem when it has been recreated to its fullest glory after Jesus returns. I can picture the scene, a great pilgrimage of God's people—every era of man, every race, every culture, joyfully traveling to Jerusalem for a great celebration. I see similarities to the pilgrimages made to Jerusalem for the holy festivals of old, such as Passover. But this will be on a much grander scale. On that journey I will be joined by my sons, my daughters, and my grandchildren; and even their descendants, if the Lord tarries that long. On that journey I will feel emotions beyond anything I've ever experienced in my life. My *"heart will throb and swell with joy."* I will be dancing and singing.

I choose to trust in this promise, confident of what lies ahead. In my dark moments, when the waves of sorrow come, I remember what God has done for me, and I remember his promises. And my hope is renewed. I will finish this chapter with a verse from the prophet Jeremiah.

Jeremiah experienced some extremely painful things in his life. In the third chapter of Lamentations, he poured forth all of his discouragements. He then said:

> *"I well remember them, and my soul was downcast within me. Yet this I call to mind and therefore I have hope: Because of the Lord's great love we are not consumed, for his compassions never fail. They are new every morning; great is thy faithfulness."*
> Lamentations 3:20-23 (NIV).

Chapter Fifteen:
Gifts for our Healing

"The Lord alone is our radiant hope and we trust in him with all our hearts.
His wraparound presence will strengthen us. As we trust, we rejoice with an
uncontained joy flowing from Yahweh! Let your love and steadfast kindness
overshadow us continually. For we trust and we wait upon you!"
Psalm 33:20-23 (TPT).

The Jews of old were afraid to even utter the name Yahweh, which at the time was simply spelled YHWH. It was too holy.

I have shared many of the wonderful things that God did to heal our broken hearts and restore our hope and trust. There was another huge gift that I have mentioned. In some respects, it was the most significant of all—the gift of our granddaughter, Teddy.

Teddy was a baby when we lost Joel. She was seven when we lost her mom. She has had her own journey of grief, that of a child losing their parent. It is hard for children to know how to grieve. Outwardly, she showed little emotions in the months that followed her mother's death. It was all bottled up.

Sometime after Jenna's death, a grade school counselor told us about Camp Erin, a camp for children who have lost loved ones. The camp was already full that year. Fortunately, Teddy was able to attend the following year.

The camp was run by Providence Hospital of Seattle and sponsored by the Jamie Moyer foundation. Jamie is an ex-Mariner baseball player and he and his wife are wonderful benefactors in the Seattle community. The Moyer's helped to start the camp after some of their friends lost a daughter to cancer. This was their way of honoring her life, and the life of her parents and siblings.

So, on the last weekend of August of 2013, Teddy went to Camp Erin. Over the course of the summer, we attended some pre-camp events ... an orientation, and a pizza feed, which were held to help people get to know one another. Teddy met a girl there who had also lost her mother. They became immediate friends.

Teddy seemed to have a good understanding of what the camp was all about. The morning she was getting ready to leave she put on one of her mom's old coats. It was oversized but perfectly fitting.

I cannot say enough good things about Camp Erin, held at the local Girl Scout campground. When the kids arrived, well-trained "buddies" greeted them to act as cabin counselors. There was a homemade quilt on their bunk, and a new Teddy Bear to sleep with. There were service dogs that woke the kids up in the morning with sloppy kisses, and put them to bed at night. The key staff were trained grief counselors who loved and supported the kids every step of the way.

The camp provided a wonderful mix of fun activities intertwined with activities purposed to help them honor and grieve for the ones they have lost. The kids were provided with many opportunities to talk about their pain and sorrow if they wanted to, but were never pressured to do so.

For Teddy, the most meaningful activity was the Love Light Ceremony. The kids created floating luminaries on a foam base. They decorated them with items which reminded them of their loved ones. That night they floated them on the lake. Teddy told us that she cried the entire time. Her emotions were obviously high because she didn't even eat any of the pizza the girl scouts made after the ceremony.

This camp provided a healing experience for Teddy. It broke down the walls she had built to protect her heart from sorrow. When we picked her up Sunday afternoon, she cried for two hours. Rhonda and I took turns sitting with her—just being there to lean on—as her pain was released from the deepest recesses of her heart.

Though Teddy had occasionally displayed her sorrow, she had shed very few tears prior to this. I had a sense she was trying to be stoic. I believe this camp was the best thing that could have happened to her. It taught her how to truly grieve. In the weeks that followed, she was more emotional, and there were more times of grieving. One particular night stands out in my memory. As I was putting her to bed, she began to cry. She told me that she was having a difficult time remembering her mom. My heart was nearly ripped from my chest.

*****

I once read something that I think applies here. The author, who had just lost his wife, mother and youngest daughter in a car accident, had a dream of trying to run after the setting sun—trying to escape the encroaching darkness. When he told a family member about his dream, they told him something that changed his entire perspective, *"The shortest route to the sun is to go east, into the darkness, towards where the sun will rise again in the morning."*

This rings true for me. You can run as hard as you can, trying to escape grieving. But sooner or later the darkness will overtake you. I believe the sooner you enter into the sorrow ... the sooner the dawn will come.

*****

Two days after camp, Teddy, Rhonda and I left for a short vacation to Lake Chelan, a beautiful, crystalline, deep-water lake in eastern Washington. It is one of our favorite places.

Teddy brought her Love Light. We stopped in Leavenworth where we'd had our family memorial the previous summer. We made our way down to the river where we had sprinkled Jenna's ashes. Teddy placed her luminary in the water, then took a stick and wrote her mom's name in the sand. She was learning how to remember ... how to honor her mother's memory ... how to reach inside and grab hold of the sadness which resided within her young heart.

Afterward, we returned to the Munchen Haus where we had celebrated Jenna's half-marathon, and gone to honor her memory after scattering her ashes. This has become a family tradition, a part of our remembering and treasuring what we have lost, and what we still have.

We had three relaxing days together at the lake. One evening after dark, Teddy took her Love Light down to the lake, turned on its battery-operated candle, and floated it upon the deep, dark waters. She kept that luminary for years, decorated with silk leaves and flowers, a pink feather, seashells, jewels, and a tiny guitar. I don't know what all of those things mean to her, but to me it became symbolic of a young heart learning to release its pain. Each time she put it on the water, a tiny bit of her pain would float away, to join with the ashes of her mother.

Psalm – You thought of me
Frank Curtiss, January 31, 2008

Long, long before
  my fleshly body
  breathed its first,
  you thought of me,
  a chosen man;
And you smiled.
I began as an idea.
  As in his mind,

a craftsman sees,
his finished work,
so you saw me,
chosen to be a son.
A humble vessel,
you made me to be.
Yet you endowed me
the wisdom of the ages;
the secret truth,
that leads to life.

You sent a man
to tell me the story,
knowing all along that I would believe.
For you had planted
a seed of faith in my heart.
May I never doubt
your heart towards me,
or deny that which
you did for my benefit;
reaching down from heaven
a hand of rescue.

How is it
that many do not see
the beauty in that hand?
The jagged scar, proof
of that which lies
within your heart.

Long, long before
  I ever thought of you,
  you thought of me.
And you smiled,
  a knowing smile,
  as you saw beyond;
  beyond the hardship
  of these days.
You saw me
  and those you gave me
  sitting at your feet,
  feeling the warmth of your smile.

Chapter Sixteen: Little-by-Little

"Little by Little, one travels far." J.R.R. Tolkien

When loss strikes unexpectedly, it seems that you'll never catch your breath. The pain is so intense and overwhelming you feel that you will never escape its grip. As time begins to pass, any change for the better is so slight that it is imperceptible. Then, one day you wake up to sunshine and see that you are doing a little better. You start finding things to be thankful for again. You smile more. You begin to see the beauty in the world around you once again. This poem, written in the midst of it, explains it better than I can say today:

A Poem: All at Once
By Frank Curtiss, July 24, 2012

All at once
My heart shattered in a thousand pieces
Could they ever be put together again?
One by one,
I pieced the scattered shards back together
Slowly, painfully, it began to take shape
It never looked the same
Some pieces didn't seem to fit
Other pieces were missing
Every now and then,

I'd find a piece swept under the carpet
Or a friend would find one I'd overlooked
Sometimes a piece would get trampled on
By some well-meaning soul trying to help
But eventually it began to resemble a heart
It still ached a lot
And occasionally a sharp pain …
   would send it into spasms
Sending me in search …
   of some way to numb the pain
But as the months passed
And the years evaporated
The pain eased a little
My face was less contorted now
Joy crossed my path more often
And though my heart was still …
   a leaky, patched up vessel
It somehow functioned …
   as a heart is supposed to
Then came the next blow
More crushing that the first
It felt as if God himself was against me
And all his promises were for naught
Despair settled over me
My old friend sorrow
   pinned me to the ground
I found myself pummeled
   by huge waves of sorrow
Hope was sucked away
   by the receding water

swept away to the depths
like the ashes of my daughter
flowed away down the river
to the vast sea of anguish
There is no way
to piece together my heart again
The pulverized pieces lay scattered
like black sand upon the shore
Can those grains of sand be melted
in the furnace of your refiner's fire?
Can they be formed into a new heart?
Maybe you have begun that process already
Some onlooker might observe
A glass heart is a transparent heart
But please be careful
For it is as delicate as crystal
Easily shattered once again

The sorrow is always there at some level. It ebbs and flows like the tide, pulled to-and-fro by memories. This was an analogy I had used for some time and then recalled it when I read in Psalm 42:

"I hear the tumult of the raging sea as your waves and surging tides sweep over me." Psalm 42:7 (NLT).

Two verses later, the psalmist (one of the descendants of Korah), goes on to say:

"O God my rock," I cry, *"why have you forgotten me? Why must I wander around in grief, oppressed by my enemies?"*
Psalm 42:9 (NLT).

But with the passing of days, I found that the times of overwhelming sorrow became less frequent and less prolonged. The times in between became happier. I found a measure of peace returning ... my countenance began to rise ... and my heart found more to be grateful for. It became easier to say, "I am good," and mean it when someone asked how I was doing.

They say that time is the great healer. I don't believe it is *time* that heals. But *over time*, God can do amazing things in our lives if we allow him.

Even within the context of our faith I have wondered at times if *healing* is the best word to use. I have only found one Bible verse that uses that word specifically in regard to grief or a broken heart. In Psalm 147, David wrote, *"He heals the broken hearted and binds up their wounds."* Psalm 147:3 (NIV).

But don't get me wrong. Even if healing is not the best word, I'm not saying that God leaves us to wallow in our pain and grief. Quite the contrary. Let's look at some other things our compassionate Father speaks to us in his Word.

In the first few verses of Isaiah, chapter 61, Isaiah prophesies that Jesus was coming to *"bind up the brokenhearted."* As I ponder that image, I can see the hands of Jesus holding my heart. He goes on to say that he would, *"comfort those that mourn and provide for those who grieve in Zion."* Even more audaciously he adds, *"to bestow on them (us) a crown of beauty instead of ashes and the oil of joy instead of mourning."*

David wrote, *"The Lord is close to the brokenhearted and saves those who are crushed in spirit."* Psalm 34:18 (NIV). In light of this, I have accepted that God does heal our hearts, so I will sometimes use that word going forward. But as with many serious wounds which are healed, scars remain behind as evidence.

I believe that a heart so crushed will always bear scars. But I do not see that as a bad thing. I believe that Jesus carries his scars with him to this day. Those scars are part of what make him beautiful—more on that later. In us, too, our scars can become a beautiful thing. They make us human. They make our hearts more tender. They make us approachable, just as Jesus' scars make him so relatable to us. And they can create compassion within our hearts, so long as we do not allow bitterness to take root.

I have a friend who was the chaplain for the police and fire departments in the city of Redmond. After the loss of our daughter, he said something to me which was difficult to hear at the time. He said he envied me having experienced such great sorrow because of how God uses it in one's life. I politely nodded, like I understood, but inside I was screaming, "How could you say such a thing? If you only knew the immensity of my pain." But over time I have seen the truth in what he said.

Look at the story of Naomi as told in the book of Ruth in the Bible. If you've never read it, I would strongly encourage you to do so. It is a beautiful story of loss and redemption.

Naomi and her family had moved to Moab during a time of famine. While living there, her husband and both of her sons died. Naomi returned to her home of origin, accompanied by her daughter-in-law, Ruth. When greeted by old friends and family, Naomi said to them, *"Don't call me Naomi. Call me Mara, because the Almighty has made my life very bitter. I went away full, but the Lord has brought me back empty."* Ruth 1: 21 (NIV).

But as the story unfolds, we see God doing a beautiful work. In Naomi's case he used her wonderful, loyal, daughter-in-law Ruth, a Moabite, and Naomi's relative Boaz, who is referred to as her kinsman redeemer, to bring about a new and wonderful chapter in her life. In the end of the story, Ruth and Boaz have married and given birth to a baby boy. Upon his arrival, Naomi takes the baby and cuddles him to her breast. Then the women of the town come and say to her:

"Praise the Lord, who has now provided a redeemer for your family! May this child be famous in Israel. May he restore your youth and care for you in your old age. For he is the son of your daughter-in-law who loves you and has been better to you than seven sons!"
Ruth 4:14,15 (NLT).

This is such a beautiful story of God restoring joy in the midst of sorrow, and turning ashes into something beautiful, as he promised in Isaiah. Not only that, but the baby Obed grew up to be the father of Jesse, who fathered King David, the man who is called, "A man after God's own heart," the man who became the author of most of the Psalms.

*****

If I had my life to do over again, and could choose my fate, I would never choose to go through the losses we have gone through—not in a million years. And yet—I am compelled to say—as promised in Psalm 34, God has drawn close to me in ways I may never have experienced otherwise. I now know what it is like to experience his comfort, and to experience joy in new and different ways. I don't think I will ever be thankful for the horrific losses we have suffered. Yet I am thankful—deeply thankful—for the work that God has done in our lives in the midst of it.

Chapter Seventeen:
The Battle Against Bitterness

"Then I realized that my heart was bitter, and I was all torn up inside. I was so foolish and ignorant—I must have seemed like a senseless animal to you. Yet I still belong to you; you hold my right hand. You guide me with your counsel, leading me to a glorious destiny. Whom have I in heaven but you? I desire you more than anything on earth."
Psalm 73:21-25 A Psalm of Asaph (NLT).

If you've ever experienced deep grief, you may have noticed that for a time life becomes a place of extremes. At least, it was for me. Even in the darkest hours there were many rich blessings in my life for which I remained extremely grateful. In one moment, I would find myself relishing time spent with my grandchildren, who have the ability to bring great joy to my heart. Or I would be out on my bike on a sunny day, enjoying the wind in my face. Both then and now I am rich with good friends, with whom I can laugh or cry. And I am blessed with an amazing woman to be my wife. Even with the loss of my children, I have come to recognize that there is great favor upon my life. God was beginning to restore my hope.

A Psalm – Hope Because I Believe
By Frank Curtiss, December 18, 2019

It is because I believe in your goodness …
Because I trust in your promises …
That I have hope

115

And hope gives me joy
Even when darkness,
   settles in upon my soul
For hope looks forward
It sees the light when my eyes cannot
Hope is the anchor for my soul
When I had none,
   you proved your goodness to me
You took my broken heart within your hands
You massaged it lovingly …
   to soften that which was brittle …
   because of my bitterness
My love for you grew,
because of your great tenderness to me
I will never forget your kindness

A couple of chapters ago I told you about the joy and healing that our granddaughter Teddy has been in our lives. I can barely find the words to describe the impact of that gift. Teddy graduated from high school last year and is now attending school at Santa Barbara City College, where she is studying art and art history. She shares an apartment with a friend. We miss having her in our home, but we talk and text regularly. We have watched her grow from a child with little confidence in her artistic abilities to a young woman, growing daily in her confidence and talent as an artist. But far beyond that, we are proud of the young woman of character she has become. She is thoughtful and compassionate and a young woman of integrity.

Another huge gift came to us nine years ago. Our second oldest son, Noah and his wife, Jenn, brought a bouncing baby boy into the world. His name is Miles and I love that kid to the end of the world and back (even though he runs circles around me on the soccer field—oh, how the tables have turned!). We are blessed!

Yet, even with these amazing blessings it would have been easy for us to take on a different attitude. We could have allowed bitterness to plant its roots in our hearts. Few people would have faulted us.

But here is what I know. Bitterness is a sad, lonely road. It creates despair and depression, and drives others away from us. Others may want to be supportive but no one can abide a bitter heart for long (except for Jesus, but it would make him very sad). Bitterness creates animosity towards God, making it nearly impossible for him to do all the wonderful work he wants to do in our lives. The writer of Hebrews had this wise insight:

"Watch over each other to make sure that no one misses the revelation of God's grace. And make sure no one lives with a root of bitterness sprouting within them which will only cause trouble and poison the hearts of many." Hebrews 12:15.

That's the thing about bitterness. Its effects are far-ranging. It's a poison that impacts us and everyone in our lives. It is a bitter root which produces bitter fruit.

It's nearly impossible not to have some bitterness in our lives. We are all prone to it, not only in times of grief but also in times of anger, when we feel we've been wronged by people, or even by God. That's one of the reasons we need each other. Notice that Hebrews said, *"Watch over each other ..."* Why? *"To make sure that no one misses the revelation of God's grace."* Our Christian faith is not meant to be walked alone. It is intended to be both a personal and corporate experience. I believe that is one of the reasons people struggled so much with hopelessness and depression during COVID-19. They were taken out of community—face-to-face community.

I personally experienced bitterness after we lost our daughter. For a time, I had little empathy for the pain or losses of others. Whatever hard things they were walking through seemed trivial compared to our loss. When our old pastor, Lee Bennett—in his

117

mid-sixties at the time—got cancer, my attitude was … *Yes, of course I want him to get better, but he has lived a full life. Something my son and daughter never got the chance to do.* While others showed great concern, I *pretended* to show that I cared. This changed over time, partly because a good mutual friend encouraged me to pray for him. I did so out of obedience, and over time God began to soften my heart. Thankfully, God brought him through his cancer and he lived another ten years before succumbing to complications from congestive heart failure. He continued to pastor for six of those years.

Today, I believe bitterness has no root in my life. God is creating a heart in me which is more like his own, a heart which *"Rejoice(s) with those who rejoice and weep(s) with those who weep."* Romans 12:15 (NKJV). I still have room to grow in this, as we all do, but God is not finished with me yet! Nor with you.

I believe that God gives us the opportunity to be his hands and feet. He uses us to help bind up the wounds of others, to show compassion and to speak words of life and love into their hearts. Thankfully, where we fall short, he shows up to fill the gap—more than fill—he overflows. One of my favorite things about God is stated in Psalm 56, where David writes:

> *"You keep track of all my sorrows. You have collected all my tears in your bottle. You have recorded each one in your book."*
> *Psalm 56:8 (NLT).*

What an incredible statement. It tells me that our tears have worth to God. Nothing is wasted on him. He uses our joy, and he uses our sorrow. He uses both blessings and hardships to make us more like himself. Yet, I believe that as we become more like him, we also become more uniquely ourselves, the people he meant us to be all along.

Chapter Eighteen:
Setting Our Feet Upon the Rock

"I waited patiently for the LORD; he turned to me and heard my cry. He lifted me out of the slimy pit, out of the mud and mire; he set my feet on a rock and gave me a firm place to stand. He put a new song in my mouth, a hymn of praise to our God. Many will see and fear the LORD and put their trust in him." Psalm 40:1,2 (NLT).

Rhonda and I dealt very differently with our grief, especially with the loss of our son Joel. I grieved very openly, bleeding my emotions over everyone. Rhonda grieved privately. At times it was difficult because she did not want to talk about it. A lot changed in the seven and a half years between the losses of Joel and Jenna.

During those years, Rhonda became involved in a ministry called Celebrate Recovery. CR—as it's often referred to—is a faith-based twelve-step program which puts greater emphasis on the power of God than other twelve-step recovery programs. Rhonda attended CR groups at a couple of different churches over the years, including our home church. After the program ended there, she began to attend a group at Overlake Christian Church in Redmond, where she served as a group leader for many years.

It is impossible to quantify how much she grew over the years. She was better prepared to face our losses head on and communicate what was in her heart. She has grown from a woman who lacked confidence and was prone to depression, into a strong, confident woman who is not afraid to step out and lead others. She is no longer involved in Celebrate Recovery but now leads a women's group at our Revive Church in Redmond. She is kind, compassionate, and a trustworthy friend to me and so many others. She has become a spiritual mom.

Because of her growth (and I like to think my own as well), things were very different when we lost our daughter. We were able to communicate our feelings and respect the different places our emotions would take us at different times. Our highs and lows were rarely in sync. As difficult as those days were, facing the pain as a couple made the weight easier to bear.

A Psalm: An Anxious Man

By Frank Curtiss, November 16, 2010

I have been an anxious man, O Lord
Where has my peace fled?
If I am standing upon you …
If you are the solid rock 'neath my feet …
Why do I feel like a drowning man …
   pulled down by the quicksand of time?
Is not all eternity before me?
And yet I see the good in this too
Pulled toward love with new urgency
Like the ocean is pulled by the moon
For eons, the earth has circled the sun
And the moon stays in its allotted course
May my life be like this, my God
Held fast by the strength of your love

*****

God was using other things in my life during these days—everyday practical things—to help me through the deepest days of my grief. I'm sharing these here—not because I think they are things you should do—but because they helped me. It is possible they will help you too. That is for you to decide.

The first is that I began a regimen of more serious exercise. When we lost our son, I turned to weightlifting. I had so much negative energy that I literally wanted to hurt someone. I needed a way to release it. I was already working out at a gym, and began to take it more seriously. I fell in with a group of guys that liked to bench press together every week. Most of these guys were far stronger and more serious about it than I was, or ever wanted to be. I was surprised that they accepted me into their group but they welcomed me with open arms (strong arms, I must add!). It's hard to describe what this did for me. It was a way for me to release my negative energy. And the endorphins which came from the lifting helped my mental attitude.

As time passed by, my focus shifted. I had been a casual bicyclist for several years and enjoyed it a great deal. Our daughter, Jenna, loved exercise and physical activity. She even worked as a trainer at a gym for a time. She loved to compete in organized events (such as the half-marathon she ran), and challenged me to consider it.

Because I enjoyed cycling, I decided to get a better bike. I bought a carbon fiber road bike and began to ride more. Seattle is a great place for this, at least for seven or eight months out of the year. I go to the gym during the off-season. There are hundreds of miles of excellent cycling trails surrounded by God's beauty.

I began to ride more and signed up for my first century ride (a hundred miles). We lost Jenna not long after that, but her encouragement remained with me. For a time, it became my motivation. It almost felt as if she were riding with me, telling me to get my butt in gear when I was dogging it. I laugh because that's the kind of woman she was.

One day when I was out riding, training for my century ride, I met a group of guys on the trail. We began to ride together. The following year they talked me into doing a ride with them known as the STP, Seattle to Portland. It is a two-hundred-mile ride. Most people do it in two days but they preferred to do it in one. I had my doubts but began to train with them. Once again, I found that this helped me release the negative energy. Spending time with these men was another gift. All of us were in our fifties or sixties and being with them was life giving.

The night before our STP ride I barely slept, worried that I wouldn't be able to make it. One of the guys picked me up at 4:00 in the morning. We met up with the others and were on our bikes before 5:00. There were times during the ride when I thought my body would give out, but that evening, around 8:00, we pulled into the park in Portland, surrounded by a crowd of cheering supporters lining the road. I felt like I was finishing the Tour de France. At times, I think about this and suspect that our arrival in heaven will be like that.

I've never done the STP since but I still love to ride. Most of the time I am able to ride with friends. Most of my rides are twenty to thirty miles, with some longer rides mixed in. A few years ago, during COVID-19, I joined a friend to do a century ride known as Obliteride, a fundraiser for Fred Hutch Cancer Research Center. I had not done a century ride since the STP and once again had my doubts. I was sixty-six years old. But we did it, in large part due to the support of friends and family, some of whom rode portions with us. We raised a lot of money. It was a true gift.

There are three reasons I ride. One is the exercise. I find it to be good for both my physical and mental health. The second is because of the friends I get to spend time with while doing a healthy activity. They are men who love God, like I do. That is also good for my emotional health. The third is that I hope it will extend my life, or at least the quality of my life. I have a strong desire to be healthy and present for my family for as many years as

I can, especially for Teddy. Rhonda and I are fifty years older than she is, and she has no mother, no siblings, and no relationship with her father. I know that God has already assigned the day of our death, but I hope to remain healthy for as many years as I am able, to be a blessing and not a burden.

I am thankful that God has given me the health to do these things. When I am out riding, with the wind in my face, surrounded by God's beauty, I feel his good pleasure.

PART THREE: ASCENDING THE HILL OF THE LORD

"Who shall ascend the hill of the Lord? And who shall stand in his holy place? He who has clean hands and a pure heart, who does not lift up his soul to what is false and does not swear deceitfully. He will receive blessing from the Lord and righteousness from the God of his salvation. Such is the generation of those who seek him, who seek the face of the God of Jacob."

Psalm 24:3-6 (ESV).

Chapter Nineteen:
The Gift of Writing Psalms

"To worship God in wonder and awe opens a fountain of life within you, empowering you to escape death's domain." Proverb 14:27 (TPT).

I'm certain some of you are asking yourself how we could ever move on with our lives … how we could find any measure of hope, and joy, and peace again after all that we have walked through. I've asked myself the same question a thousand times. When I first began to recognize God's goodness and blessing in our lives again, I found myself feeling guilty about it. But I knew that was not what God wanted. It was a lie coming from the enemy, and a denial of God's power to restore. I also knew that neither my son nor daughter would want that for us. They did not do what they did to punish us.

In the introduction to this book, I explained some of the reasons I write psalms. God has done so many things to restore us. I have tried to yield myself to his healing scalpel. For me, writing psalms has been one of those things—an integral part of my healing.

I love the Biblical Psalms. I appreciate their honesty. I love what they teach me about the nature of God. I am in awe of how they prophesied the coming of the Messiah and his suffering. And I love that I can find reflections of my own heart in the words of David, Asaph, and the other writers. Most of us do not look to the Psalms for instruction. We look to them for strength and encouragement.

126

Probably the most significant reason I began to write psalms was because—like King David—I desired to be a man after God's own heart. I accepted Jesus as my redeemer and became born again on New Year's Eve 1972 in a little Baptist church, twenty-two days after marrying Rhonda. We were barely nineteen.

But for years afterward I struggled to live out my faith the way I believed God wanted me to. I was immature, driven by the desires of my flesh. As a result, I almost gave up on my faith—not because I stopped believing—but because I didn't think I could walk the walk. I stopped believing in myself.

Writing psalms has been an immeasurable gift to me. Paul, in his letter to the Ephesians, wrote, *"Speak to one another with psalms, hymns, and spiritual songs."* (Eph. 5:19) Another reason I love to write psalms is that it draws me into the very presence of God. David longed for that presence above all else. When I write psalms, I become more aware of his presence. My relationship with him grows in intimacy. I hear his voice more clearly. He encourages me, strengthens me, and comforts me. And I am able to articulate the thoughts of my own heart with greater clarity. The Holy Spirit gives me greater understanding of myself, my desires, my fears, and my deep yearning to become more like Jesus. I begin to see myself through his eyes. This psalm is an example:

Have I Created God?
Frank Curtiss, July 30, 2010

Have I created God in my image?
Have I sifted through the words of life,
Choosing only those which make me feel safe?
Some of the words are hard to eat
I chew on them but cannot swallow
Is it pride that drives this insanity
Or fear of the one I cannot tame?

That Lion who hails from Judah
Fiercely stalking the souls of men
Pouncing upon them with his love
In the night time – while most men sleep
I wrestle with him
Yet I cannot overpower his strength
Exhausted, I collapse upon my bed
I slumber a while
Then, in the stillness that comes before dawn
I awaken to a whisper,
a quiet voice drifting upon the night
"Come along child that I love,
Come and I will teach you.
Let us walk the winding path together,
and I will open your blind eyes.
Your ears will burn;
your spirit will leap with joy.
Your countenance will be radiant,
with each new discovery.
I have put on flesh,
that I might be found by you.
Sit in stillness at my feet,
Rest upon that gentle slope
Which overlooks the sea
and hear my words which give life"
I take a deep breath
My heart is encouraged by God's affection
But my mind continues to reel
At questions still unsolved
Then… as if they'd been floating on the air

Some lost words come back to me
Words recently spoken by a brother...
"The greatest day of my life
Was when I learned to embrace
The mysteries of God."
I chew on that a while
Buffeted by the implications
Trying hard to take it in
Is there freedom to be found
Within this simple thought?
Can I find rest in those words?
Then the quiet voice of the dawn
Comes to me again...
"Do not judge yourself harshly,
for what you have yet to learn of me
No man is able to understand
All that... I Am
But do not fear
I have set aside eternity,
for you to know my thoughts
Draw near to me my son
Set your heart and mind on peace
For I have been found by you"

As I write my prayers, my gratitude, and honestly express my emotions, my heart is drawn into worship. I begin to see the glory of God, the essence of who he is. As I write, I try to listen to his voice, translated to me by his Holy Spirit, and write what I hear. When I listen with an open heart, it begins to transform the pathway of my thinking. I become more grateful, seeing all that I have to be thankful for, even in the midst of hard times. My faith is affirmed. My trust grows. I become more hopeful. And though he satiates my soul with all these good things, I become hungry and thirsty for even more of him. That is one of those dichotomies of faith. The more we have of him, the more we hunger for even more. The fire in our soul burns hotter and hotter. We continually long for fresh touches of his love.

Let's read again the question David asked in Psalm 24:

> *"Who may ascend the hill of the Lord? And who shall stand in his holy place? He who has clean hands and a pure heart, who does not lift up his soul to what is false and does not swear deceitfully. He will receive blessing from the Lord and righteousness from the God of his salvation. Such is the generation of those who seek him, who seek the face of the God of Jacob."* Psalm 24:3-6 (ESV).

I see three parts in this: David's question. The answer to his question. And the blessing that comes from our obedience.

The hill of the Lord referred to here is likely Mount Zion, where David had set up his tabernacle. David established this tabernacle in the very midst of his kingdom, a place to make God the center of all things. David employed thousands of musicians, singers and others to maintain worship in his tabernacle. The worship never ceased and the fire on the altar never went out. It is because of David's great love and devotion that Jesus, our eternal King, chose to come from his lineage.

Like David, I long to ascend the hill of the Lord. Aside from his cleansing, my heart would not be pure. But because of all he has done for me, I am worthy. I ascend with joy and laughter, and I ascend with tears. For it is he who invites me in any and all circumstances.

Which brings me to the final reason I write psalms. For me, it has become part of my living out my role as a priest of the Lord. Yes, I am called to be a priest. So are you. In the book of Isaiah, he prophesied that this would come to pass. He writes, *"And you*

will be called priests of the Lord, you will be named ministers of our God."
Isaiah 61:6 (NIV).

Peter later confirmed our priesthood, writing:

"But you are a chosen people, a royal priesthood, a holy nation, God's special possession, that you may declare the praises of him who called you out of darkness into his glorious light."
1 Peter 2:9 (NIV).

The book of Revelation confirms this again in its first chapter, where it says:

"To him who loves us and has freed us from our sins by his blood and has made us to be a kingdom of priests to serve his God and Father—to him be glory and power for ever and ever! Amen."
Revelation 1:5-6 (NIV).

There is so much in these verses. We are called chosen, God's special possession. We are called part of the royal family, part of a holy nation, called out of darkness into his glorious light. All of this was accomplished because Jesus shed his blood to free us from the power of darkness and sin. And we are told that our role is to be priests of the most-high God. Our role is first and foremost to serve him—to minister to the Father, declaring his praises, and to give him glory—then also to represent him to the people.

Part of my royal priesthood is to worship him. When musicians sing to the Lord, or lead others in worship, they are living out their priestly calling. I am sad to say that God did not bless me with musical talent. I love music! I'm hoping in heaven he will bless me with musical abilities. One desire I've expressed to God is that my son, Joel, will teach me to play guitar when we are together once again. But God did give me other talents I can use for his glory. He has given me the ability to create works of art, and to write. And so, I do these things for his glory.

Chapter Twenty: Writing Psalms … an Honest Endeavor

On a few occasions, I have had the opportunity to teach classes on how to write psalms. At our old church, I did a weekly workshop with a small, talented group of writers, most of whom were more talented than I. At our current church, I was given the honor of teaching it on a congregational level on Wednesday evenings.

I encourage everyone to give it a try. You might just find that it does for you that which it has done for me. If it is of no interest to you, feel free to skip this chapter. But if you want to give it a try, here are some things to consider in the process.

First, I would encourage you to make yourself a student of the Biblical Psalms. Don't just read them … study them. Look at their structure, their content, and the different writing techniques utilized.

Most people think of David when they think of the Psalms. He did write at least half of those within the psalter. Some Psalms have no author identified, so the exact count is undetermined. There were at least seven different authors that we know of, each with his own unique voice. There are also many additional Psalms (or songs) in other parts of the Bible, such as in Exodus 15 ("The Song of Moses and Miriam"), Judges 5 ("The Song of Deborah"), and 1 Samuel 2 ("The Song of Hannah"), to name a few.

I tell you this to encourage you to find your own voice, your own true self. I have a few friends who write psalms. One of those friends is Steve. Stylistically, his psalms are very different from mine. I love the way they express his uniqueness and the hunger for more of God within his heart.

Let me tell you how I personally begin when writing a Psalm:

- I start with a single thought, or idea. It can be about God, or about myself (in relation to him), or even about the congregation of God.

- I write that down and then try to listen to what the Spirit of God is speaking. Sometimes I feel like I hear him well, and am very inspired. Other times it's a struggle. That's okay. There is value in all of it.

The Power of Honesty:

I believe one of the most important traits of a psalm is honesty. David wrote, *"You have looked deep into my heart, Lord, and you know all about me."* Psalm 139:1 (CEV). Maybe this is why David felt so free to be honest with God. I believe that when we are fully vulnerable before God, open and unafraid, we discover our truest identity. We find a freedom to be ourselves. What good is it to hide our feelings and emotions from God when he knows it all? It is futile. We are only fooling ourselves. In my experience, when we confess our feelings and emotions to him, we find greater freedom. And he can take our negative emotions and turn them into praise for his glory.

Doubt is another issue which we all face, if we're honest. Even after all God has done for me, I have experienced times of doubting his goodness, his love, or even his very existence.

In the Psalms, I see I am not alone in my doubts. In Psalm 13:1, David wrote, *"How long will you forget me? Forever? How long will you look the other way?"* (NLT). In Psalm 22:1, he said, *"My God, my God, why have you forsaken me?"* This, of course, turned out to be a prophetic writing, as these words were spoken by Jesus on the cross. As with our emotions, God is fully aware of our doubts, so I see no reason to hide them. By expressing them honestly, we allow God to redeem them, to restore our faith.

Not only are the Psalms a good place to express these emotions and doubts, but they are a good place to admit to our sins and shortcomings. Along with that, they are a perfect place to repent of those. Writing these things down has a way of solidifying our repentance, at least it does for me. Instead of "covering up" my sins, I can bring them to Jesus and let him "cover over" my sins with his blood.

The Power of Thankfulness and Praise:

I have heard it said that God will not come close to the bitter heart. There is probably truth in this. I believe he always stands ready. Even when we are bitter. But in our moments of bitterness, we hold him at an arm's distance.

Rhonda and I could have allowed ourselves to become consumed by bitterness. We had our moments. But living there only brings misery. I only know one way out of a bitter spirit. That is thankfulness and praise, two of the most powerful forces in the world. As we acknowledge the things God has done in our lives in thankfulness and praise, it also increases our faith.

Those things were nearly impossible for me in the hardest days following our losses. At times, it took a Herculean effort to see the bright side of anything. But God, in his faithfulness, surrounded us with such a loving community that it was nearly impossible not to be thankful for those people, and to see them reflecting God's goodness.

For me, an important factor in all of this is that I did not *want* to become a bitter person. I wanted to find solid footing again. I had a granddaughter to raise, sons who needed a steadfast father, and a wife who needed my love and support.

Don't misunderstand me. I believed it was important to live transparently before them. Putting on a false front for others is a lousy way to live and grieve. It does none of us any good. So, whatever thankfulness I managed to muster up had to be genuine.

When life assails us, when it tries to drown us in sorrow and bitter feelings, how does one get from here to there? I believe that thankfulness must come first, then praise will follow. It is the natural course of life.

So how do you come back to that place of thankfulness? In part, it is a matter of our will, but it is also a work of the Holy Spirit. As far as the will goes, *desiring* to live a life of thankfulness is a good start. Then, choosing needs to follow our desire.

There are certain things we can do to help the process. In my journaling I established a habit of writing down things I was thankful for. Frequently, I would write down *"Three things I am thankful for."* I tried not to be repetitive day to day in what I would write. Then, throughout the day, I would look for things. It is amazing how many can be found if we allow ourselves to see them.

I also wrote words of thankfulness into the psalms I was writing—even when I wasn't feeling it—even when all I wanted to do was scream at God. Choosing to do so involves God in the process.

Here is a psalm of thanks I wrote less than two years after we lost Joel:

A Psalm: Discovering Joy in Praise
By Frank Curtiss, August 21, 2006

My heart discovers joy
When my lips praise you, Jesus
When I say "thank you, Abba Father"
  for all your mighty deeds
    when my lips speak your praise
      my heart follows after
It recognizes, yes, God is worthy
  worthy to be worshipped and exalted

I just as easily, maybe more so
   go to a place of grumbling
My eyes dwell on those things
   which challenge my faith
Those things which create
   pain and heartache
Then worry and fear consume me
My heart grows restless within
But then, O Lord, you speak to me
The soft voice of your Spirit
   comes to remind me …
"Praise God, and trust in his promises,
Believe in him who causes
   all things to work for your good."
And so I praise you my God
I turn my eyes to you in worship
My redeemer and friend
He who calms the roaring seas
Who speaks to my heart,
   "Peace be still!"

Another way I involved God in the process was to pray and ask him, not only to comfort me in my sorrows, but to return to me a thankful heart. In my experience, when we ask for such a thing, especially something so clearly within his will, he always answers. It can take time—particularly when God is working with a stubborn old mule like me—but he is faithful to do his part. He opens our eyes to see his goodness all around us. That can only be done by his Spirit at work in us. Without him, all we see is darkness.

There is one other thing that is key, in my view; that is spending time in God's Word. His written Word is a constant reminder of his goodness, and his desire for us to live in joy and thankfulness. To the people of Thessalonica, Paul writes:

> *"Rejoice always and delight in your faith; be unceasing and persistent in prayer; in every situation [no matter what the circumstances] be thankful and continually give thanks to God; for this is the will of God for you in Christ Jesus."* 1 Thessalonians 5:16-18 (AMP).

Does this feel like an impossible assignment? Sure, it can feel that way, especially when we are in difficult circumstances. But if we meet him along this path, if we take even a single step in obedience, he will come and meet us. He will take us on a journey to this place. So, hang out with Jesus, spend time studying his Word. And pray. And when you find yourselves in a tough place in life, I would suggest always including the Psalms in your daily reading.

Chapter Twenty-one:
Thankfulness and Praise
in the Psalms

Sing joyfully to the LORD, you righteous;
it is fitting for the upright to praise him.
Praise the LORD with the harp;
make music to him on the ten-stringed lyre.
Sing to him a new song;
play skillfully, and shout for joy.
For the word of the LORD is right and true;
he is faithful in all he does.
The LORD loves righteousness and justice;
the earth is full of his unfailing love.

Psalm 33:1-5 (NIV)

Some Psalms are almost entirely praise. Psalm 33 is a beautiful example. It goes on for 22 verses of nothing but praise. Many Psalms express difficulty in situations, or emotions such as sadness, despair, feelings of abandonment, or anger (at God or others). Yet, even in the most honest of these you will nearly always see a turning point to praise.

Psalm 28 is an interesting example of this. In verse 1, David says:

"Do not turn a deaf ear to me. For if you are silent, I might as well give up and die" (NLT).

Five verses later he says:

"Praise the Lord, for he has heard my cry for mercy. The Lord is my strength and my shield. I trust him with all my heart" (NLT).

What a huge shift in outlook and attitude!

If you want to see an even more dramatic example, read Lamentations, chapter 3, which reads like a Psalm. I mentioned this in my intro. For twenty verses, the mighty prophet, Jeremiah, tells God all of the wrong he has brought upon him. Here is a brief excerpt:

"Like a bear lying in wait, like a lion in hiding, he dragged me from the path and mangled me and left me without help. He drew his bow and made me the target of his arrows. He pierced my heart with arrows from his quiver." Lamentations 3:10-12 (NIV).

The language is rich and full of powerful imagery. I can feel Jeremiah's pain and relate to how he feels. Then, beginning in verse 21, we see the dramatic shift:

"Yet this I call to mind and therefore I have hope: Because of the Lord's great love we are not consumed, for his compassions never fail. They are new every morning; great is thy faithfulness!" Lamentations 3:21-23 (NIV).

I love these pivotal shifts even more than I love the honesty of difficult emotions. Why? Because they affirm the goodness of God to me. They reassure me of his faithfulness and compassion in the midst of our human difficulties. They tell me all the things he is to me: my rock, my fortress, a sun and a shield, the lover of my soul. They remind me that he is faithful and can be trusted with my heart. Therefore, I have hope.

Even the most optimistic among us become discouraged. Whining can come easily to us in these times. I know it does for me. It is at those moments when we most need to turn our hearts toward praise. We need to remind ourselves of who God is, all that he has done for us, and all that we have to be thankful for. We all need this affirmation. To read it changes how we think ... the very pathway of our thinking. Brain science confirms this. I believe this is what the Apostle Paul was talking about in Romans 12:2 when he said, *"Do not be conformed to the pattern of this world, but be transformed by the renewing of your mind"* (NIV).

Yes, reading it is useful. Speaking it is even more so. For me, writing it has an even more powerful effect on my mind and heart. Here is an example:

A Psalm: Of Joy You Speak

Frank Curtiss, September 2006

Of joy you speak to my heart …
"Have joy, for Yeshua reigns!
His heart is towards you.
He pursues you upon the hills.
He searches for you among the glens."
Though I try to hide
   there is no escaping his love.
Tirelessly he carries me
   after he has worn me out.
He takes me to a quiet place,
   where his voice is all I hear.
He tells me of the good things
   he has done for me.
And gives me a glimpse
   of the joys which lie ahead.
I love you O Yeshua,
   my bright and morning star.

Throughout the remainder of this book, I will provide tips and suggestions on writing psalms. I hope you will consider giving it a try.

Chapter Twenty-two: The Psalms are Prayers

"Now restore us again, O God of our salvation. Put aside your anger against us once more. Will you be angry with us always? Will you prolong your wrath to all generations? Won't you revive us again, so your people can rejoice in you? Show us your unfailing love, O Lord, and grant us your salvation."
Psalm 85:4-7 (NLT).

One of the beautiful things about the Psalms is that most of them are honest, heartfelt prayers, as we see above. They teach us how to pray in any and every circumstance: sorrow, joy, faith, doubt, when we have sinned and need mercy, and when we are walking in thankfulness. They give voice to the entire anatomy of our souls: from *despair* (Psalm 88) to *joy* (Psalm 20:4,5 and Psalm 126).

Some of the Psalms model *communal* prayer, such as the verses in Psalm 85 above. Notice the use of the word *us* which is used multiple times.

Other Psalms model *individual* prayer for us. Psalm 13, written by David, is a good example of this:

"O Lord. How long will you forget me? Forever? How long will you look the other way? How long must I struggle with anguish in my soul, with sorrow in my heart every day?" Psalm 13:1-2 (NLT).

Notice that David was not afraid to question God. This is common in the Psalms. Is God offended by our questions? Apparently not. He includes these Psalms in his Word. Even after all of David's questioning, God continues to call him a man after his own heart.

141

Here is a prayerful psalm I wrote:

A Psalm – Longing to See You Face to Face
Frank Curtiss, September 30, 2016

My heart longs for you, O God!
I see you from a distance
But I long to see you face to face
I see reflections of you
Then they disappear
I long to touch your face
I yearn to place my hand in yours
I wish to hear your voice
Speaking comfort and love to me
Where can I meet with you God?
Must I wait 'til heaven
    to be held in your arms?
You promised to be with me
You tell me
    that you dwell inside of me
Moses was able to come
    into your holy presence
His face radiated your glory
Where can I find you O God?
Where is a place
    where I can hear your voice?
I long for a quiet place
A place of still waters
Where the only sound I hear
    is your voice whispering to me

Quiet my heart Yahweh

Quiet the voices in my mind

Shut out the cares of this world

'til all that is left is you and I

Awaken me

   that I will not miss your voice

Speak to me words of love

Poems of delight

Take joy in me

And help me to delight in all you are

I suppose it is possible to cross the line in our questioning. But if we love God, and desire to please him, I believe that the worst-case-scenario is that he may correct us, as he did Job. Job questioned God's fairness and apparently went a little too far. God called him on the carpet—so to speak. Yet God called Job the most righteous man that ever lived, and he went on to restore and bless him greatly again after the great trials he allowed Satan to place in his life (Job, chapters 38-42).

Every night before I go to sleep, I read out of the Psalms. I am surprised how often I find the cry of my own heart within them. Often, these express troubles that I didn't even know how to say with my own words.

I recently finished watching season three of *The Chosen* which I thoroughly enjoyed. Many episodes touched me. One that hit particularly close to home was the final episode of season three. In the previous episode we were made aware that Peter was extremely angry with Jesus. While Jesus was tending to the needs of others, Peter and his wife, Eden, were grieving deeply over a stillborn birth which took place while Peter was away with Jesus. This part of the story was a fictional interpretation, yet it drove home the story so effectively. As they recounted the story, they were doing flashbacks to Asaph, who was a priest in David's tabernacle. Asaph was reading Psalm 77 (one of several Psalms he wrote) before King David. It is a very honest Psalm. The first three verses read as follows:

"I cry aloud to God, aloud to God, and he will hear me. In the day of my trouble, I seek the Lord; in the night, my hand is stretched out without wearying; my soul refuses to be comforted. When I remember God, I moan; when I meditate my spirit faints. Selah"
Psalm 77:1-3 (ESV).

Because of the sorrows we have walked through, my heart made a strong connection to this Psalm and to the anguish in Peter's heart, and to his anger toward Jesus. I remember reading this Psalm after the loss of our daughter and how it spoke what my heart was feeling, especially where it says, *"my soul refuses to be comforted."* Those words spoke exactly how I felt. I didn't think I would ever get past the pain. I remember praying the words of this Psalm. It was one tiny step in the process of God comforting my soul. Part of it was knowing that others before me had felt such desperation and brought their brokenness honestly before God.

Let me share the rest of the Psalm with you. I am leaving it in paragraph form:

"You hold my eyelids open; I am so troubled that I cannot speak. I consider the days of old, the years long ago. I said, "Let me remember my song in the night; let me meditate in my heart." Then my spirit did a diligent search: "Will the Lord spurn forever, and never again be favorable? Has his steadfast love forever ceased? Are his promises at an end for all time? Has God forgotten to be gracious? Has he in his anger shut up his compassion?" Selah

Then I said, "I will appeal to this, to the years of the right hand of the most high." I will remember the deeds of the Lord; yes, I will remember your wonders of old. I will ponder all your work, and meditate on your mighty deeds. Your way O God, is holy. What God is great like our God? You are the God who works wonders; you have made known your might among the peoples. You with your arm redeemed your people, the children of Jacob and Joseph. Selah

When the waters saw you, O God, when the waters saw you they were afraid; indeed the deep trembled. The clouds poured out water; the skies gave forth thunder; your arrow flashed on every side. The crash of your thunder was in the whirlwind; your lightnings lighted up the world; the earth trembled and shook. Your way was through the sea, your path through the great waters; yet your footprints were unseen. You led your people like a flock by the hand of Moses and Aaron." Psalm 77:4-20 (ESV).

I think you will agree that this is a powerful, heartfelt, and honest Psalm. I don't know what had taken place in Asaph's life to bring him to this place. But clearly, he had gone through the deep waters, and had seen his people go through them as well. Not all of it reads as a prayer of supplication. Other verses read as a conversation he is having with himself. Other parts read as a conversation with God, which is still a form of prayer.

Prayer at its best has a rhythm of call and response. Two good examples of this are in Psalms 12 and 50. In both of these, David is complaining about how the godly and faithful are vanishing because of the sinful acts of others. In both of these, the Lord replies in similar ways. In Psalm 50, God replies:

"Because the poor are plundered, because the needy groan, I will now arise. I will protect them from those who malign them."

In the following verse David adds:

"And the words of the Lord are flawless, like silver purified in a crucible, like gold refined seven times." Psalm 50:5-6 (NIV).

What I love about these is that David is both speaking (*writing* actually) and listening. He is listening to hear God's voice. We would do well to do the same. It takes a quieting of the heart and mind to do so.

So, the Psalms are a wonderful tool to assist us in our own prayer life. Some can simply be prayed word for word. Others may take a change of language to fit your context or situation. Either way, I would encourage you to pray the Psalms as well as other prayers within the Word, especially when you find yourself struggling with your prayer life (something I often do). I would also encourage you to write your own prayerful psalms. It's an easy way to get started. Just pour out your heart honestly before God— no matter where it is at in that moment in time.

Chapter Twenty-three: Back in Time … Where My Faith Story Began

"The Lord alone is our radiant hope and we trust in him with all our hearts. His wraparound presence will strengthen us. As we trust, we rejoice with an uncontained joy flowing from Yahweh! Let your hope and steadfast kindness overshadow us continually, for we trust and we wait upon you!"
Psalm 33:20-22 (TPT).

How does a man obtain faith? What brings him to trust? How does he come to hope in God? I suppose these are the million-dollar questions. If I knew the answers, I would probably be a great evangelist. All I can really tell you is what the Word of God says, and speak from my own experience.

I have already shared many of the things God did in my life to restore my faith and trust, and renew my hope. But for them to be rebuilt and restored, they must have existed in the first place. Let me share the story of how I came to faith.

I believe that God invites us all to respond to him and become children of faith. But he also gave us all a free will. He did not—does not—want robots. He wants hearts that love him of their own volition. He continually calls us to himself, continually knocks on the doors of our hearts. He searches for us when we are lost. But it is up to us to respond.

A Psalm: You Have Hemmed Me In

By Frank Curtiss, June 26, 2003
I turned to my left and saw the Lord
To my right and he was there
I turned and looked behind me
He was there as well
My attention turned ahead
Was he to be found there as well?
Then my heart was comforted
For there in the path he stood
The Lord had hemmed me in
He protects me from the rear
He guards my flank always
He never wearies or abandons his post
He goes ahead to make my way straight
He calls out to me, "This is the way."
"Come near and follow me."
Shall I follow him? The road may be difficult
Yet, what choice do I have?
What other roads can I take?
The other roads entice me
But I know where they lead
Why do I fear the difficult road?
He has always been with me
When it has become too hard for me
He has carried me in his arms
O my heart, trust in the Lord
He has never led you astray
Follow him on the path of life
Fix your eyes on he who saved you!

I was the youngest of five siblings. We did not attend church much. My parents got divorced when I was six. My mom Gladys was a wonderful, strong woman, but she had her own struggles with faith. We would go to church for short periods of time, a few weeks, a few months, and then stop. Still somehow, I began to respond to God at an early age. I remember reading a Bible storybook when I was ten years old. It made an impression on me and planted seeds in my heart.

When I was twelve or thirteen, my mom remarried. Paul was a man's man, an oil man from Wyoming. He loved fishing, hunting, camping, and hiking. He had two sons and twin daughters of his own who often lived with their mother in Wyoming. Having not had much of a father, I was not formed from the same mold as Paul. I think he thought I was kind of soft. I don't remember feeling fully accepted by him, but I loved and respected him all the same.

Some months after they married, they had planned to take a road trip for their honeymoon. They rented a camping trailer and were heading north from Southern California to do a western loop through California, Oregon, Idaho, Yellowstone Park, southern Wyoming, and then home through Utah, Nevada, and Arizona. Days before they left, I broke my arm. They decided to take me with them instead of leaving me in the care of my older brothers. I doubt that having me along was the honeymoon of their dreams, but it turned out to be a memorable trip for me.

Late one afternoon, as we were passing through the redwood country of Northern California near Klamath Falls, we came upon a tourist attraction called Trees of Mystery. It looked intriguing, so I talked them into stopping. They let me go in alone. I'm sure they wanted some time to themselves.

The golden hour began to settle over the woods as I explored the mysteries of this Redwood Forest. I don't really know what triggered the experience that came next. Suddenly and unexpectedly, I became aware of God's presence. In that moment

I knew that he was real. I can only describe it as God's Spirit descending on me in this place of beauty, overwhelming me with a sense of awe. A few years later I had a similar experience as I was hiking in the Sierra Nevada Mountains with some friends.

Over the next few years, some very difficult things occurred. In 1968, my brother Jody (third in the birth order), was killed in Vietnam, just days before he was scheduled to return home. I was fourteen. I had always looked up to Jody, who was eight years older than me. He had been a very loving and supportive big brother.

Sometime after that, my mom and Paul separated. He went back to Wyoming for work. While he was there, he was working beneath his car when the jack gave way and he was crushed to death. These deaths, especially that of my brother, Jody, were extremely difficult. It was a time to grieve.

Aside from those tragedies, I had many wonderful memories of my growing up years. We moved to downtown Huntington Beach after my parents divorced. HB was a small town in those days, a wonderful place to grow up in the sixties and seventies. We lived in apartments and house rentals. My mom worked as a grocery checker to support us. She worked hard but barely eked out enough to make ends meet. My older siblings got jobs to help out. We didn't have a lot. I shared a bedroom with my three older brothers, and even our sister for a time. We never felt poor though. That life was not abnormal in those days, and our home was rich in love.

I had a close group of friends. We attended Huntington Beach High School, and spent our summers hanging out at the beach. I loved art, and showed some talent. I took advanced art classes in school. When I turned sixteen, I got a job at the local McDonald's and bought my first car, a baby-blue '64 Ford Galaxy. It was a tank and guzzled gas like one. Luckily, gas only cost $.25 a gallon.

I was a compliant child at home, never giving my mom any trouble. Away from home, things were different. Nothing terribly crazy. We drank beer and smoked weed. I let my hair grow long and went to rock concerts. Since long hair was not allowed at McDonald's, I wore a short-hair wig to work under my paper hat.

I graduated high school in 1972. I was planning to spend that summer on Catalina Island. My best friend's parents had bought an old hotel on the island that they were renovating. My plans changed, however, when my manager told me they were planning to promote me to assistant manager. Looking back now, I think it was fate, because a week or two later a cute little blonde named Rhonda walked in, looking for a job. A few weeks later I asked her out. Our first date was to the beach. I fell head over heels. A few months later, at a drive-in theatre, after watching *Fiddler on the Roof*, I asked her to marry me. She said yes!

Rhonda got cold feet a few weeks later and almost backed out of our engagement, because I wasn't yet a Christian. She had been raised in a Baptist church. Her parents were going through a divorce that had turned her world upside down, and she was struggling with her faith. Still, I could see that it was real to her and I assured her that I was willing to explore faith more deeply. We started attending a little Freewill Baptist Church in Garden Grove with her older sister Ruby Kay and husband.

Rhonda's dad gave us $500 and told us we could spend it however we wanted on our wedding or honeymoon. We decided on a small family wedding in her family's living room. We married on December 9, four days after I turned nineteen. We took a three-day honeymoon to Santa Barbara and Solvang. We used what was left of the money to make a deposit on our first apartment. Yes, the cost of living really was that much less in the early seventies!

I have a memory of one night in the living room of our little apartment. Rhonda was talking to me about her faith. Through tears, I told her that I'd heard only 144,000 would make it to heaven and that there was no way I could be good enough. She stared at me, puzzled, then assured me that was not the case. Somewhere along the line, I had been exposed to some Jehovah's

Witness teaching (it was their theology at that time, which was later reversed).

A couple of weeks later, we attended the New Year's Eve service at that little Freewill Baptist Church. There was a testimony time. One in particular moved my heart, given by an elderly woman (elderly by my nineteen-year-old perspective—not by my current age). Her faith and her love of God were so genuine, it pushed me over the edge. When the altar call came, I was the first one there.

I wish I could tell you that I walked a straight line from there to here. I had made two covenants within weeks of one another—one to Rhonda, and one to God. I broke them both. I desperately wanted to walk in faithfulness but struggled mightily. Sexual sin was my Achilles heel. I turned left, right, went backwards and forwards.

But I can tell you this, that once God got ahold of me, he was never going to let me go. No matter how stupid I was being, he never stopped loving me, nor calling me back home.

Chapter Twenty-four:
My Early Days of Faith

A Psalm: I Am Your Great Reward

By Frank Curtiss, September 12, 2010

The thought comes to me
As if floating on the night air
Carried upon angels wings
Whispered by the Spirit of God
"I am your great reward"
I know this is no new thought
God spoke these words to Abraham
I've read it many times
But never before has it come to life
Carried its power to my soul
Its meaning was obscure to me
But no longer …
"I am your great reward"
I think of what it means
"I Am"
God is …
Jesus is …
The Spirit is …
They are alive

They always were
Always will be
My spirit quickens
"I Am ... your ... great reward"
"Your ..."
That's me
God gives himself to me
Nothing held back in cautious reserve
Waiting to see if I can be trusted
No, only love is poured forth
I feel his pleasure
His affectionate smile
The twinkle in his eye
"I Am ... your ... great reward"
Great ... not small, nothing lacking
Complete, total, all in, all in
His great love, his faithfulness
Mercies ... unearned, undeserved
Yet lavishly bestowed
"I Am ... your ... great reward"
"I Am" your prize
"I Am" the purpose of your life
The very reason you live and breathe
Every good thing is part of me
All that is grace and beauty
Every noble thought and deed
Everything good, all blessings
Pressed down ... overflowing
"For you. Yes from me ... to you.
I am your great reward!"

Rhonda and I recently went to see the *Jesus Revolution* movie with a group of friends from church. We loved the movie. It was a trip down memory lane for us. By no means were we in the center of the Jesus movement of the early seventies. But we were touched by it.

During the first few years of our marriage, Rhonda and I attended the small Freewill Baptist Church in Garden Grove, California, where I was saved. Occasionally, we would go to one of the weekly concerts held in the huge tent of Calvary Chapel in Costa Mesa. Later, when Calvary moved into their big new building, friends began to invite us to some of their teaching events. It was there that we first began to learn about the Holy Spirit. This was all new to us. We felt so much life there, so much freedom.

Speaking of life, in 1975 Rhonda gave birth to our first son, Christopher. I believe I floated out of the hospital, ten feet off the ground. Shortly afterward, we made the decision to attend "Big Calvary" as we called it. I remember the night we had our Baptist pastor over to share the news. He tried to convince us that the Holy Spirit no longer imparted gifts to his people as he had in the days of the apostles. We no longer accepted that as the truth.

Attending Calvary was a breath of fresh air. Pastor Chuck Smith was a man full of joy and an amazing Bible teacher. Our faith grew. The only downside was that it was a church of several thousand people by then. After being there for a year, we decided that we needed to find a home group to become better connected. We looked at the bulletin board and saw that there was a group meeting in Huntington Beach, so we decided to check it out. When we arrived, we found the house bursting at the seams. We found a few square feet of floor to sit on. Pastor Steve Purdue was another excellent teacher. We discovered that they were planning to start a Calvary Chapel in Huntington Beach. We decided to join them.

That summer the church met in Lake Park, just blocks from where I'd grown up. When autumn came, the church moved into

Dwyer Junior High School where I had gone to school. Those were good years. We bought our first home, a small condominium, and I was promoted to head manager of the McDonald's I was working at in Huntington Beach. A year later they transferred me to the McDonald's on Coast Highway in Newport Beach, owned by the same family. In 1978, God blessed us with a second son, Noah. What a gift.

We were in a wonderful church and my job was going well, but in the midst of it we got a bug to move north to Washington State. In hindsight, I have to assume it was God's doing. We knew two couples who had moved up, and at the time it was a far more affordable place to buy a home (not true anymore). We were outgrowing our little condo and the houses in Orange County were out of our price range. We took a trip up and visited our friends, one couple in Woodinville, another on Whidbey Island. We loved it and decided to make the move. We sold our condominium in California, packed up our VW bus, and headed north. We bought our first house on a third of an acre in the rural community of Woodinville.

In California I worked for a McDonald's franchisee. Here, I took a job with McDonald's Corporation. They placed me in a restaurant in downtown Seattle. It was not an easy place to work. We had to deal with gangs, drug addicts, pimps and prostitutes. It felt like a hostile foreign territory to a suburban boy like me.

We did not find any churches we liked in Woodinville, so we drove into Seattle to attend the Calvary Chapel for a few months. Not wanting to make the drive more than once a week, we helped to start a bible study group with our friends (and their friends, and their friends). Within weeks, it grew to more than a couple of dozen people. Quite a few of us were California transplants who had attended a Calvary Chapel or Vineyard church. Within months, we knew we wanted to start a church. One of the couples knew a pastor, Lee Bennett, who had been a pastor on staff with Chuck Smith at Calvary Chapel, and then with Chuck's son, Chuck

Jr., at Calvary Chapel of Dana Point. Lee and his wife Sue came to visit and the next thing we knew we had a real live church that became known as Calvary Northshore.

Before Lee and Sue returned to SoCal to pack up their belongings, he asked the members of our group to choose elders from among us. I was chosen at the ripe old age of twenty-five. I felt honored, but in hindsight (always 20/20 vision), I would not recommend this for anyone! I will keep the next several years brief. The church thrived but I did not. Not spiritually, anyway.

In 1981, God blessed us with the gift of another boy, our third son, Joel. A few years later, Rhonda decided it was time to stop having children. Oops! Too late. A week later we found out she was already pregnant. In 1985, God blessed us with Jenna, our one and only girl!

My career was doing fine but our marriage was going through rocky waters. Rhonda was struggling with times of depression, and for years I had been struggling with pornography, sexual sin, and improper relationships. I knew there was no way I could continue as an elder. I stepped down and after a time we left the church. For ten years we attended a large Foursquare Church. In some ways, I was thriving. In other ways, my life was faltering.

I believe it was about 1991 when our marriage came to the crisis point. I seriously considered leaving Rhonda but knew I had so much to lose. And I think I knew my faith would not survive. I made a good choice. I chose my Rhonda, I chose my children, and I chose Jesus all over again.

Chapter Twenty-five:
The Long Road Home

Psalm – Is it right for a man to challenge you?
Frank Curtiss, Sept. 10, 2007

My Father
  who dwells in heaven.
I have made my desires
  known to you.
Indeed, you have known them all along.
None of my desires are evil O lord.
They are only for fullness of life;
  life for me,
  life for those I love.
Is it right for a man to challenge you?
To ask that you make your power known?
To remind you of your promises?
Jeremiah did so,
  Moses and David.
Yet you were displeased with Job,
  when he questioned your fairness.
I could try to hide my feelings of doubt;
  try to disguise my fears;
  that my prayers will ever be answered.

But you O God know my heart.
To what purpose would a man cover over,
  that which is laid bare before your eyes?
And yet you desire more of me,
  faith, hope, trust;
  belief in your goodness and power;
  indeed, confidence that you even exist,
  and you care about the plight of man.
Oh that by my own power,
  I could bring these things about,
  that I could know that I know.
My heart relies on you O God,
  for the very power to believe.
Be patient with me, my God.
Do not be silent because of my unbelief.
For you have placed your Spirit within me,
  to remind me of your goodness.
Your spirit, which is holy
  speaks oh so quietly.
I hear your voice in the morning.
"Be at peace, my good and faithful servant.
My work is not yet complete".
Praise be to my God!
May I delight in you all of my days.
Open my eyes to see your Spirits touch.
Quicken my spirit to praise you,
  for that which is not yet complete,
  knowing that your promises to me are true.
In you God I place my trust.
You are my only hope.

When I first re-committed my life to God, I felt that my faith was in many ways stronger. I had counted the cost all over again. But I came with the attitude that I would be a sideline observer. It seemed to me that when I had put myself on the front line of the battle, the enemy (yes, his name is Satan) had taken me down. I felt that if I just went to church and quietly believed, I would be better off.

I shared this with a friend one day. He looked me in the eye and gently said, "Sounds like Satan has you right where he wants you." It was like he took a 2x4 and knocked me upside the head. He was right.

Once again, I wish I could tell you that I did everything right from here, but addictions are difficult to overcome. I was doing better, but would still stumble at times.

During these days, another key dynamic came into play. My career had been relatively successful. For the last several years I had been in mid-management, first as a supervisor of corporate-owned McDonald's, then as a field consultant working with franchise owners, then as a training consultant, teaching classes to managers. But I was discontent in my career. I was traveling a fair amount, which was hard on Rhonda and not healthy for a man struggling with sexual sin. And I had never liked the corporate games and politics of climbing over people (or them climbing over me) to get ahead.

I also had an entrepreneurial spirit itching to launch out on my own. I considered several options. Restaurants are hard work and the failure rates are high. But it was the business I knew best and I was confident in my knowledge and skills. So, after much consideration, and discussion with Rhonda, we decided to pursue our dream.

Our favorite food to eat was pizza, so we decided to launch our own place. I spent a couple of years in preparation, working on recipes, preparing a business plan, and looking for a location. In 1993, we opened Frankie's Pizza & Pasta in an old building originally built as an Arctic Circle Hamburger restaurant in downtown Redmond, Washington.

Not only was I out of the corporate environment and travel, but I was now working with my family. It put me in a place of accountability. It was the best thing that could have happened to me. On top of that, we were successful. To put it simply, I had designed Frankie's as a place that I would like to eat at with my family, hoping that others would too. We aimed for the sweet spot between the everyday pizzeria and fine dining, a place with great food and wine, affordable prices, a nice atmosphere, and friendly service. We tagged ourselves *"Your Friendly Neighborhood Italian Café."* We did not get rich but we made a decent living. We were open for twenty-four years until our landlord sold the property to a developer.

A few years after opening Frankie's we returned to our old church. Prior to our leaving, they had chosen to follow the Vineyard Church movement which was born out of Calvary Chapel. Later, during our absence, they opted out of the Vineyard and became a non-denominational church, known as Northwest Community Church. After returning, we remained for twenty-four years. They were our family of faith. It was a place where people were encouraged to be genuine and transparent. We needed that environment. I've told you how difficult the teenage years were with our family, and the losses which followed. Without our church family at our side, I don't know how we would have survived.

The sad part is that over the years the church had to relocate several times and also went through a couple of difficult splits. What had once been a thriving congregation of a thousand, shrank to a couple of hundred. Our pastor, Lee Bennett, was aging and had not been successful in establishing a successor. The church shut its doors in 2019, thirty-nine years after it had begun.

In the year that followed, we tried a couple of different churches. One was a mid-sized church that Rhonda and I liked;

but our granddaughter, Teddy, was not connecting. It was important to us to have her in a place where she could thrive, so we joined a large church where some of her friends attended. Rhonda had been involved in their Celebrate Recovery program for years, so she also knew many people. I went along and tried my best to make connections. Then COVID-19 hit and you all know what happened. The church went to online services. Nothing was the same.

But God had a wonderful future in store for us. In the spring of 2020, Rhonda was on her morning walk when she noticed that a church near to our house was holding an outdoor service in their parking lot. Hungry for fellowship, we decided to check it out the following week. We had lived near this church for almost twenty years. For some reason, I thought of it as an old fuddy-duddy church with no life. That may have been true at one time, but recently we had heard great things. They turned out to be true.

It took me about five minutes to realize we had found our new home. We've never been happier in a church. No church is perfect but Revive Church is a thriving body with leaders and people who are all-in. They take God's Word at its word, believing it all to be true. The worship is deep, and the teaching is exceptional. We have developed deep bonds in our three years there. And God has used it tremendously to continue our journey of healing and falling more deeply in love with Jesus. The icing on the cake is it is about a quarter mile from our house. We usually walk to church, rejoicing as we do so.

Chapter Twenty-six:
A Greater Understanding of the Biblical Psalms

A Psalm: The Gentle Breeze of the Spirit

By Frank Curtiss, July 31, 2010

The spirit blows, a gentle breeze
  as upon the Sea of Galilee
If I unfurl my sail
  the wind will take me
  where ere the Spirit wills
But oft I fight the wind
My sails I lash to the mast,
  fearing what adventure
  the Spirit will take me on
Or I sail against The Wind,
  tacking to and fro,
  hoping The Wind will take me
  to the safety of the sheltered cove
Exhausted I arrive there
I toss my anchor into the still water
Yet this silent cove of isolation
  where I've come to hide from God
  is not the place of rest I had hoped

I perspire in the warm air
   which seems not to move
I am parched with thirst
   but fear to drink the stagnant water
Hungry, I throw my nets over the side
   they come back to me empty
The water ripples gently, as the Spirit
   invites me to pull up my anchor
I wish the ears of my heart
   could hear him better;
   that I could trust the voice within
But he speaks in a whisper
   barely audible at times
   only when my heart is still
But I am afraid
I've heard him wrong before
I know he is beckoning
Yet fingers of terror grip my heart
I beg to know where
   the Spirit desires to take me
But all he says is *"Come.*
 Pull up your anchor.
 Raise your sails.
 "Let me fill the canvas,
   like a gentle wind.
Place your hand upon the tiller.
Hold it gently.
Let the wind guide you,
   its power unseen, except by its effect…
   clouds skittering by… a gull soaring
   though its wings are unmoving"

So I ask myself,
   do I possess the courage
   to sail to places unknown?
Do I trust the Spirit
   who shrouds my future in mystery?
What harrowing storms will I face
   if I sail the open water?
Will my faith falter
   when my boat is tossed and battered
   by storms which rage upon the open sea?
I feel the gentle breeze again
   caressing my face,
   like the fingers of a lover.
Such tenderness melts my resistance.
My soul trembles,
   whether from fear or excitement
   I no longer care
For if I remain
   in this hidden cove of safety,
   my perishing will be slow,
   and who will see but God
So I choose to follow
   that beckoning whisper,
   for even if assaulted by storm
   I have one who sails with me
   One who can quiet the storm
   (though I may have to wake him)
Or who knows
Maybe I'll even step out of the boat
   and risk the waves afoot

If you are going to try your hand at writing psalms, I think it is good to have a deeper understanding of the Psalms within God's Word. As I have mentioned already, I am a student of the Psalms, partly because I find them to be a rich addition to my understanding of God and of my own heart, and partly because I like to use them as a model for my own writing.

When I first started to write psalms, I wrote them solely for myself and for God. In the beginning, they looked and sounded very much like the Biblical Psalms. Over time—as I have grown in my writing—I have begun to share my psalms for the benefit of others, and my writing style has changed. My psalms are developing their own uniqueness. One of my goals is to bring a fresh *rhema* word, using language easily understood by today's world. I have no desire to mirror our culture, which has strayed so far from God, but I do desire to portray God in such a way that anyone in today's world can see and experience his goodness for themselves.

Having said this, I still believe in having the original Psalms as an anchor for my own writing. Keeping this in mind, let's take a deeper look at the different types of Biblical Psalms. As I describe these to you, be aware that few Psalms are entirely of one nature or type. Most interweave these various elements. Here are a few of the most common:

Imprecatory Psalms: These are Psalms that *imprecate*, or invoke judgment, calamity or curses upon one's enemies or those perceived as the enemies of God. David wrote a number of these. A couple of examples are Psalms 58 and 69. In Psalm 58, after describing all of the wrong his enemies are doing, David writes:

> *"Break the teeth in their mouths, O God; LORD, tear out the fangs of those lions! Let them vanish like water that flows away; when they draw the bow, let their arrows fall short. May they be like a slug that melts away as it moves along, like a stillborn child that never sees the sun."* Psalm 58:6-8 (NIV).

David uses some pretty graphic language here … *"tear out the fangs of those lions,"* and *"may they be like a slug that melts away."* As a gardener living in a damp climate, I had to smile at that one. I hate slugs! I do all the work, digging up the soil, amending it, fertilizing it, planting seeds, and pulling weeds. Then they come along and try to eat it all. This year they destroyed my sugar snap peas. Aargh!

Usually, imprecatory Psalms are not my favorite. I'm not sure that I would wish a slimy, slug-like death on anyone, and yet I must admit that at times, when I see extreme injustice, they take on new meaning. Other times, when I have strongly felt the attacks of the enemy, these have given language to my prayers.

Psalms of Thanksgiving, Praise, and Worship: These Psalms affirm to us who God is and his attributes. I won't spend a lot of time here since I wrote about it earlier. Psalm 111 is a beautiful example. Look at how many wonderful things it tells us about God's character in just a few short verses:

> *"He has caused his wonders to be remembered; the LORD is gracious and compassionate. He provides food for those who fear him; he remembers his covenant forever.*
>
> *He has shown his people the power of his works, giving them the lands of other nations. The works of his hands are faithful and just; all his precepts are trustworthy.*
>
> *They are established for ever and ever, enacted in faithfulness and uprightness. He provided redemption for his people; he ordained his covenant forever—holy and awesome is his name."*
> Psalm 111:4-9 (NLT).

Wisdom Psalms: Wisdom Psalms are meant to be *instructive,* either from man to man, or God to man. Psalm 37 is one of my favorites and a perfect example of a wisdom Psalm. Pay attention to these instructions, as well as to the blessings promised if we follow them:

*"Trust in the L*ORD *and do good; dwell in the land and enjoy safe pasture. Take delight in the L*ORD*, and he will give you the desires of your heart.*

*Commit your way to the L*ORD*; trust in him and he will do this:*

*He will make your righteous reward shine like the dawn, your vindication like the noonday sun. Be still before the L*ORD *and wait patiently for him; do not fret when people succeed in their ways, when they carry out their wicked schemes."* Psalm 37:3-7 (NIV).

I count about eight instructions here on how to live in a place of great blessing.

Lament Psalms: These Psalms express our *human* struggles of anguish, depression, heartbrokenness, and injustice. They often include complaints against God and even questioning his fairness, justice or mercy. In Psalm 6, David wrote:

"I am worn out from my groaning. All night long I flood my bed with weeping and drench my couch with tears. My eyes grow weak with sorrow; they fail because of all my foes."
Psalm 6:6,7 (NIV).

This is a very honest Psalm. We are not told what the specific circumstances were that led to this lament, but later he says, *"There are so many enemies who come against me."*

Later, in Psalm 22, David wrote a lament that was prophetic. You'll recognize the first line as words that Jesus would later speak out when hanging upon the cross:

"My God, my God, why have you forsaken me? Why are you so far from saving me, so far from my cries of anguish? My God, I cry out by day, but you do not answer, by night, but I find no rest."
Psalm 22:1,2 (NIV).

Notice David's questioning of God here … Why? Why? Even Jesus questioned the Father as he hung in great anguish on that rough wooden cross.

Another extremely honest lament is in Psalm 88, written by a man known as Heman the Ezrahite. Here is a small portion:

> *"You have put me in the lowest pit, in the darkest depths. Your wrath lies heavily on me; you have overwhelmed me with all your waves. You have taken from me my closest friends and have made me repulsive to them. I am confined and cannot escape; my eyes are dim with grief. I call to you, LORD, every day; I spread out my hands to you."*
>
> Psalm 88:6-10 (NIV).

Despite all of his laments he goes on to say, *"Lord, you are the God who saves me."*

Prophetic Psalms: Prophetic Psalms look into the future. David is not generally called a prophet, and yet many of his Psalms painted an amazingly accurate portrayal of Jesus. Psalm 22 above was one of many prophecies that were fulfilled. Some of them also clearly look forward to his second coming and the Kingdom of God upon the new heaven and new earth. Heman the Ezrahite, who wrote such an honest lament above, also wrote Psalm 89, fifty-two verses which paint one of the most beautiful, prophetic pictures in all of scripture. Within that, he said:

> *"I will declare that your love stands firm forever,*
> *that you have established your faithfulness in heaven itself.*
> *You said, "I have made a covenant with my chosen one,*
> *I have sworn to David my servant,*
> *'I will establish your line forever*
> *and make your throne firm through all generations."*
>
> Psalm 89:2-4 (NIV).

I hope that this little bit of knowledge of the one hundred and fifty Psalms within the Bible will give you the courage to write your own and give you license to explore varying styles and approaches. Don't worry about what others might think of them. Just begin by writing solely for yourself and for God.

Near the beginning of the next chapter, you will find one of my most prophetic psalms, which I have titled *The Psalm of the Prodigals*.

Chapter Twenty-seven: Seeing the Heart of Our Father

One evening last autumn, I attended a Sunday evening prayer service at our church. Each week a different topic is chosen for prayer. On this particular evening, we were praying for the prodigals.

For the privacy of those I love, I do not want to share details, but I will say that there are many prodigals in our lives, both among our descendants and other close family who once walked with God and are not currently pursuing their faith. This has brought sorrow to us and I would often become discouraged at not seeing answers to our prayers. But God is restoring my trust. He is continually reminding me of his many promises regarding our children and how he promises to answer our prayers. As I sat in this prayer service, I felt the Holy Spirit speak to me and I began to write. The words just kept coming. This is what he gave me:

The Psalm of the Prodigals
By Frank Curtiss, November 2022

Yeshua says...
Every road leads back to me.
The darkest highway
   has a light at the end.
I am that lamp burning bright.
I walk before them.
I hem them in behind.

I have never left them.
Nor will they be forgotten.
I am the shepherd
  who seeks the lost lambs.
I will never give up
  until all are found.
My light cannot be overshadowed.
The darkness shall not overcome it.
Every lie will be exposed.
My truth will be victorious.
My beauty cannot be hidden.
It shines brighter than the sun.
They will be drawn to my light.
Every prodigal will come home.
They will lift their eyes
  and see me running to them,
    rejoicing and singing with every step
    as joy overcomes every sorrow.
Remember my promises
  on the day your hope fails.
When your faith gives way
  and your strength is gone.
My promises are not dependent
  on any human strength.
They are mine alone to keep.
For I am the faithful one
  who answers every cry of your heart.
For it is my perfect will
  that every son be found, and
  every daughter brought home to me.

This psalm is full of hope. Because its promises are so bold and audacious, I shared it with our pastor. I wanted to be certain that I had heard God rightly before sharing it. He confirmed and blessed it, believing that it was a genuine *rhema* word from the Father. I sincerely hope that it gives you the same hope that it has given to me.

This psalm reveals to me the heart of the Father towards his children. Lee Bennett, the man who was our pastor for nearly three decades, spoke constantly of the Father Heart of God. It was the very core of his message. You would think that after hearing this message repeated a hundred different ways that it would have sunk in. It did to a large degree, so I find myself surprised when God continues to reveal it to me in new ways.

A few months later, in a Wednesday evening service, we were given time in small groups to pray in response to the teaching. I found myself in a group of four, which included a wonderful woman, Vivian, who is part of our home group. Each group chose what they wanted to pray about. I don't recall much about the teaching that Wednesday night, but it ignited something God was already doing in my heart. God was making his Word and his promises very personal. I was learning to hear his voice in his written Word as if it were spoken directly to me … and to take him at his Word. That resonated with the others, so we pursued it in our prayers.

As we gathered in a small circle, I recall Vivian's prayer. It was one of the most intimate prayers I have ever heard. I wish I could remember her exact words, though its effect on me came not only from the words she spoke, but from her gentle confidence in her relationship with her loving Father. I doubt that I can do it justice, but I am going to try. It went something like this:

"Abba … Daddy, all that you say to us is true. I know your words are true. You never lie to your children. I believe every word you speak. You have never lied to me. I believe what you say because you are my Daddy, my good, good Father, and I trust every word you speak."

I think her prayer was longer than this, but this is what I can remember without becoming repetitive. It is hard to describe the effect it had on me. This simple prayer reinforced to me the intimacy we can have with our God. It touched the deepest places inside me.

I am reminded of a passage I recently read in the Psalms:

> *"We put our hope in the Lord. He is our help and our shield. In him our hearts rejoice, for we trust in his holy name. Let your unfailing love surround us, Lord, for our hope is in you alone."*
> Psalm 33:20-22 (NLT).

Before we move on, let's take one last look at writing psalms, and consider the power of creative language.

Chapter Twenty-eight: The Power of Creative Language

A Psalm: "Grafted in the Vine of Yeshua"
Frank Curtiss, March 28, 2008

Part 1:

You have grafted me in O Lord
   to that perfect vine.
The vine is strong.
Through suffering its roots
   have gone deep.
By hardship they struggled
   through layers of rock and clay,
   'til they found the good soil;
   and the underground river
   which runs through the valley
I need no roots of my own,
   for I abide in the vine;
   that perfect rootstock.
In times of drought,
   my leaves shall be green.

During the great tempest,
   though my branches are
   whipped and tattered …
   they shall survive.
For the vine which holds
   them is strong.
The graft was made by
   the Master Gardener,
   God Almighty himself.

The Bible is full of creatively rich and beautiful language. Looking deeper into the book of Psalms, we see that the psalmists describe God to us—and illustrate how God sees us—using phrases which paint pictures in our minds. This gives us a deeper and richer understanding.

Imagery is a highly effective and emotional means of communication. That is why a good storyteller attempts to evoke mental images in the mind. The mind responds more readily to language that seems to "be" experience than to language that "describes" an experience. A good rule of any writing is to *show*, not *tell*.

Our pastor, Todd Puckett, often uses the phrases "holy imagination, or "sanctified imagination." God has created us with our imaginations. He did this for a reason. We can do a great many things with that gift. We can create beautiful works of art and music. But we can also employ it for imagining him, imagining heaven, and picturing Biblical scenes that we are reading. When we employ our imagination—allowing it to be sanctified by him, we can help ourselves and others to visualize his goodness and glory for themselves.

If you choose to write psalms or poetry, I encourage you to reach into your sanctified imagination and see what unique language you can find to paint pictures of who God is to you, and how he sees you and the world around you.

If you've ever taken a creative writing course, some of what I am about to cover may seem very basic. But it is always good to refresh ourselves and to see examples of how David and the other psalmists portrayed God and his creation.

In Psalm 42, the psalmist writes:

"As the deer pants for streams of water, so my soul pants for you, my God." Psalm 42:1 (NIV).

Can you imagine it without this beautiful imagery? What if he had simply written, *"My soul deeply desires you. I thirst for you, God"*? It is still meaningful, but not memorable. A few verses later he writes:

"Deep calls to deep in the roar of your waterfalls; all your waves and breakers have swept over me." Psalm 42:7 (NIV).

This statement is more challenging. I love the imagery but found myself perplexed whenever I read it. There is a certain mystery which surrounds it. That is not a bad thing. It's good if we occasionally have to mull over what is written. Good poetry is like that. I have my own ideas of what the psalmist is trying to say to us here but I want to let you explore its deeper meaning in your own life with the help of the Holy Spirit. He may show you something completely different, yet no less true.

Sadly, some of the literary devices used in the poetry of the Psalms are lost on us due to the language translation and our lack of understanding of the culture at the time they were written. It takes a deeper study to reveal them. Here, I will focus on those which are most evident to us: similes, metaphors, parallelisms, and hyperbole.

Let's look at these tools one at a time and see how they can help you express your *holy imagination*. You will find examples of all of these in the psalter.

Similes: A simile makes a comparison between two things, typically by using the words *like* or *as*. Here are a few examples:

> *"They are like trees planted along the riverbank, bearing fruit each season."* Psalm 1:3 (NLT).

> *"My heart is sick like withered grass."* Psalm 102:4 (NLT).

> *"I am like an owl of the desert; like a little owl in a far-off wilderness."* Psalm 102:6 (NLT).

I particularly like that last one. It invokes a sense of loneliness to me, that I believe the psalmist was feeling.

Metaphors: A metaphor is something symbolic of something else, usually something abstract. When the psalmist writes, *"All your waves and breakers have swept over me."* This is not a literal thing. The waves and breakers are a metaphor.

Here are a few other examples from the NLT.:

> *"The Lord is my shepherd."* Psalm 23:1

> *"The Lord is my rock, my fortress, and my savior."* Psalm 18:2

> *"… he flew, soaring on the wings of the wind."* Psalm 18:10

We know that the Lord is not a literal shepherd. Nor literally a rock or a fortress. But these images help us to understand his role in our lives. I love the imagery of that last one. The wind has no physical wings but it paints a beautiful picture in my mind.

Parallelisms: A parallelism draws a parallel between two similar things. Often, this is done through repetition, saying the same thing in two or more ways. Here are a few examples:

> *"The Lord Almighty is with us; the God of Jacob is our fortress."* Psalm 46:7 (NIV).

> *"Blessed is the one who does not walk in step with the wicked or stand in the way that sinners take."* Psalm 1:1 (NIV).

Parallelisms by nature are usually *synonymous,* as seen above, but they can also be *antithetical,* showing opposites. The contrast gives us greater understanding. Here is an example from Psalm 37:

> *"For those who are evil will be destroyed, but those who hope in the Lord will inherit the land."* Psalm 37:9 (NIV).

Hyperbole: Is a wonderful literary device which uses exaggerated claims or statements, not intended to be taken literally, to drive home a point. Here are two examples from the Psalms and one beautiful image from the book of Job:

> *"All night long I flood my bed with weeping and drench my couch with tears."* Psalm 6:6 (NIV).

> *"For he spoke and stirred up a tempest that lifted high the waves. They mounted up to the heavens and went down to the depths; in their peril their courage melted away."* Psalm 107:26 (NIV).

> *"When the Almighty was still with me and my children were around me, when my path was drenched with cream and the rock poured out for me streams of oil."* Job 29:6 (NIV).

Job really knew how to paint a picture with words!

One last thought: if you decide to write psalms, decide upon the perspective you will be writing from (who it is that is speaking), and to whom it will be written. It can be from *you* to *God,* or *God* to *you* (prophetic words of love and encouragement). Or it can be from you to others (the congregation), or from God to others (again prophetically, for giving strength and encouragement). It is okay to interweave them. You will see this frequently in the Psalms.

Here is part two of the above psalm. Once again, I hope you will give it a try. Many blessings to you on this journey:

A Psalm: "Grafted in the Vine of Yeshua"

Part 2:

My fruit, O Lord, is not my own.
If not for a robust vine,
   my clusters would shrivel
   and die in the summer heat.
But you, my gardener
   know how to tend the vine.
You prune the branches
   which are unruly,
   those which bear poor grapes.
You train my tendril upon the trellis,
   a perfect canopy.
My fruit hangs fully exposed,
   to the ripening rays of your son.
Not all seasons are fruitful,
   but all are necessary.
In autumn, those branches
   which bore fruit, die away.
In winter, the gardener walks.
   among his vineyard …
   pruning away the dead wood.
In spring, life erupts anew.
First, the bud shows itself.
And after the rains of spring,
   verdant leaves break forth.
But oh, the glory
   that follows in summer.
Ripe, juicy clusters pile high in the crusher.
For the Master Gardener …
   is also the master winemaker.

Chapter Twenty-nine: The Beauty of Jesus

A Psalm: Show Me Your Beauty

By Frank Curtiss, March 16, 2022

Yeshua, show me your beauty ...
You have captured me with your eyes
Transfixed me with your gaze
I peer deep within your soul
Your eyes smile back at me
Filled with passionate longing
Love, stronger than the grave
Deeper than the tumultuous sea
You invite me to follow you
To meet you in the secret place
'Neath the branches of the tree of life
Where you heal my broken soul
My heart throbs, it swells with joy
I am made whole in your eyes
Held captive by your freedom

I've related the story about how Rhonda and I ended up at Revive Church a few years ago. There are three simple words on the church's sign and website which describe their vision ... *"Pursuing His Presence."* The pursuit of him is at the heart of the church we now call home.

I started to hear an emphasis at Revive that took my heart down new paths in my own pursuit of him. Over and over, I heard the phrase *beholding his beauty*. This is not new language. David used it in Psalm 27. But in my decades as a Christian, it was language I had heard only occasionally.

The idea of *the beauty of Jesus* used to create some confusion in my mind because of the prophetic passage in Isaiah which speaks about the coming Messiah.

> *"For before him he grew up like a young plant, like a root out of dry ground. He was not well-formed or especially handsome; we saw him, but his appearance did not attract us."* Isaiah 53:2 (CJB).

Based on this description, I believe it is safe to say that Jesus was an average-looking guy as far as his human appearance goes. This makes sense to me. Sort of. Part of me thinks he should have come as a tall, handsome, man's man, with charisma and kingly bearing—someone that everyone would be drawn to. After all, he was the Son of God, creator of the universe, a member of the Trinity, one with the Father.

I am guessing that is what the Jews were looking for in their king. But the Jesus who showed up was not at all who they were expecting. He did not come to conquer Rome and establish his earthly kingdom at that moment in history. He came to be a humble servant, a teacher who would help them understand the true heart of the Father. He came to be a sacrifice for our sins. And though he was God in fleshly form, he came with the intent of being human among us, someone whom we could all relate to. The title he most often used for himself was Son of Man. Though he was God, he wanted us to be able to relate to him as a man.

So, if he was just an average-looking guy, what did they mean by *the beauty of Jesus?* And why does it matter? I would have had a difficult time answering that a few years ago. I knew that it had to mean more than his physical beauty, but my understanding was limited. I was trying to put new wine in my old wine skin.

I have learned so much about his beauty since then. At first, it was as an understanding in my mind and intellect. But that will only take you so far in the realm of faith. Now, I feel like my heart is truly beginning to see the immensity of his beauty. I know the depth of my understanding is still woefully incomplete, but I have tasted enough to know I want more. I want to fully experience his beauty, even while knowing that—like many of the mysteries of God—we will never understand it fully until we see him face to face. Still, I know that my hunger and thirst is from him. He wants us to pursue him. It was that deep yearning that inspired the prayerful psalm which I opened this chapter with.

So, back to the question, why does it matter? I am seeing people all around me experiencing the same thing I am, but I can truly only speak for myself.

For me, beholding the beauty of Jesus has undone me. It has melted my heart. The stony places are becoming flesh.

I feel like I will never be the same. It has satisfied my soul in ways difficult to describe, and yet created a deep yearning all at the same time. It has brought greater healing and allowed me to experience joy that I never thought possible after all that has happened to us. It has created a greater sense of awe. It has given me a desire to worship him more, a desire to live for him more. All things said, I believe God is using it to exchange my *ashes for his beauty*, and to make me more like himself.

It has also transformed my relationship with God the Father, who placed his beauty in the Son to fascinate us. The beauty of Yeshua is infinitely superior to all other beauty—everything that he has created—because Yeshua embodies everything the Father is. All other beauty pales in comparison. Jesus defines all that is beautiful. All other beauty is but a reflection of his own.

For me, the more I behold his beauty, the more deeply I fall in love with him. And that is what he wants from us, just as you desire your children to love you if you are a parent. But remember, it is not his outward beauty of which I am speaking.

We've all heard the phrase *beauty is only skin deep*. That is certainly true of physical outward beauty. We've all met those people who are pleasing to the eye until we get to know them. Then, we see the inconsistencies between their outward beauty and their countenance, that which reflects their inner person. We've also all met those people who look rather ordinary but exude a deep inner beauty. But the beauty of Jesus goes beyond that. In the following chapter I am going to try to describe it to you, but I suspect my words will fall short … way short.

Yet like any good desire of our heart, I know God will honor it. That is a promise he made; a promise I have found to be true in my own life. I am beginning to see his beauty more clearly than I ever have. And I am confident that as I seek his face I will continue to grow in understanding.

Chapter Thirty:
How Can I Describe?

"One thing I ask of the Lord, this only do I seek: that I may dwell in the house of the Lord all the days of my life, to gaze on the beauty of the Lord and to seek him in his temple." Psalm 27:4 (NIV).

I find that we are in good company when we recognize the beauty of Jesus. King David, the man after God's own heart, wrote the verse above. Notice the language, *"One thing,"* and *"this only."* His choice of words tells us a great deal about his life and character. To gaze upon the beauty of the Lord was his first priority. David had an intimacy with the Lord that God greatly honored. It is my heart's desire to partake of that same fruit of intimacy. More and more he is inviting me to do so. The more I eat of it, the greater becomes my desire for more.

Again, in Psalm 96:9, David wrote, *"Worship the Lord in the beauty of his holiness."* (NKJV). Some translations substitute the word *"splendor"* for beauty. Either word works for me.

Our pastor, Todd Puckett, recently made the following statement in a Sunday morning message, *"The glory of God is the essence of God."* I wrote it down because it sounded profound. I still believe it is. It's a good starting point, but now as I write it, it sounds a little esoteric to me. What does it mean? Let me share my thoughts.

I considered starting our journey of discovering the beauty of Jesus with the description that the Apostle John gives us in the book of Revelation. There, John does his best to describe the majesty and holiness of Jesus in the throne room of heaven, using human words. We will go there later. First, I want to lay a different foundation. It is time to apply the holy, sanctified imagination God has given us so that we can see all that he is. Below is a psalm I recently wrote exploring this question:

A Psalm – How Can I Describe?

By Frank Curtiss, June 1, 2023

How does one describe the beauty of Jesus?
The words have not been invented
It is indescribable, unfathomable
The train of your glory fills the temple
The beauty of your heart alone
   is more than I can grasp
The heart of your Abba Father
   inherited from the one true God
A heart that yearns for your children
A heart that is broken for us
   because it bore our every sorrow
Yet the light of your joy
   overwhelms every sorrow
As the light of dawn
   overwhelms the darkness of night
You rise up on our behalf
   as the sun rises
   casting forth its radiance
Still, such a description
   falls pitifully short
Woe is me to even think
   that I could describe

Yet you call me blessed
You've given me eyes to behold
Your fire of love ignites a fire in me
But can any man speak of such things?
You have hid them in my heart
So deep, deep within
But I long to be a river
    carrying your beauty to all the earth
Even a glimpse imparts life
Give me words O God
To open the eyes of those
    whose hearts long for you
To tear back the veil
So that you, the spotless pure one
    might be seen in all your radiance
    the beauty of the one and only savior
Reveal your beauty
Make me a messenger
If my heart carries
    a single drop of your blood
One sip of the wine
    of your passionate love
My heart will be unable
    to hold it within me
May my fruit be sweet
    upon your beautiful vine

When contemplating the beauty of Jesus, I think a good place to begin our journey is by reminding us of the scars which he bears, the scars he was rewarded when he willingly went to the cross, and all of the torture that led up to it. The Bible does not specifically tell us that Jesus still bears these scars but it is hinted at strongly. We know that when Jesus came to the apostles following his resurrection that those scars remained on his resurrected body (John 20:26-28). When Thomas experienced his moment of doubt, Jesus showed him the holes in his hands and told him to put his hand in the wound in his side. Later, in the heavenly scene in Revelation, John describes Jesus appearing as *"the Lamb who had been slain"* (Revelation 5:6). The Amplified version of the Bible goes so far as to say, *"I saw a Lamb (Christ) standing, [bearing scars and wounds] as though it had been slain."*

Thomas was able to behold the holes in Jesus' hands and his side. I believe his other scars will be just as evident when we see him. When we bow down to worship at his feet, I believe we will see the scars from the spikes that pierced them. And if we get an opportunity to see his back, we may well see the unsightly scars from the deep scourging that tore hunks of flesh from his body. Next to his hands I think that the most noticeable scars will be the ones upon his brow where thorns were driven deep within. It will be hard to miss them when we look into his eyes.

Some of you might think me insane when I describe Jesus' scars as a thing of beauty. Maybe I am. But if so, it is because his immense love has driven me there. And having experienced that love, I no longer care what man thinks of me. Sure, those scars are ugly … yet they are the most beautiful thing at the same time! Beautiful because they are there to remind us of the immeasurable suffering he went through for you and me. A deeper suffering than we will ever grasp. They will be a constant reminder of the greatest act of love ever undertaken.

The next thing I find deeply beautiful about Jesus are his eyes—eyes which reflect his deep love and compassion—eyes that search my soul and love me anyway—eyes that invite me into his presence. How can I say such a thing, having never seen him face to face? I stand by my statement. I've already shown you significant scriptural evidence of his compassion—which you probably knew anyway. And I have told you of my own experiences. If I had not experienced his compassionate love firsthand, I could not be authoring this book.

How could such deep love and compassion not show forth in his eyes? Our eyes are the window to our souls ... and we are made in his image. Yet I believe that when we look into those eyes, we will see so much more than his love and compassion. We will see the full range of his emotions on display.

In the Spirit I have seen those eyes. They dance with joy and laughter because his fatherly love always sees the best in us, and takes joy in even our smallest steps toward him. They show the passionate affection of a groom desiring his bride—eagerly anticipating being with us. Yet they also show sadness for the choices we make which take us down paths that lead to death instead of life. He yearns for us to experience the rich, abundant life he has for us, a life filled with his joy, his peace, and seeing his beauty reflected all around us. It saddens his heart when we reject him or choose those things which are inferior. I would be remiss if I did not tell you that those same eyes also flash with anger— anger at Satan when he steals, robs, and destroys—and anger at us when we show cruelty to others. God feels nearly every emotion that we do, with the exception of despair and hopelessness, for he knows the end of the story.

When we finally meet him eye to eye, what I look forward to most is seeing his eyes sparkle with affection and delight. I'm sure they already do when we come to him with hearts wide open. In those same eyes I see purity. The purity of his overwhelming goodness, and of a faithful, longsuffering, undying love, love that never breaks his Word to us. In that purity I see the light of life itself. And I see eternity.

All of this of course is a reflection of his heart. We cannot see inside a person's heart, that which beats within their chest. But the evidence is written all over them, in their eyes, in their smile, in their body language. I suppose the word *countenance* describes it best.

I feel like we have only begun to scratch the surface of the transcendent beauty of Jesus. It is a beauty reflected in his character, in all that he is and everything that he does. We see his beauty as he smiles upon us with unthinkable grace and mercy. We see it in his arms that are always open to receive his children, always ready to forgive. We see it in his deep desire to not only see each one of us saved, but to see us healed and walking in wholeness. He longs to see us delivered from oppression because he is a savior who loves justice. For that very reason he conquered death for us. We see his beauty reflected in the plans he makes for us, plans to give us a hope and a future. I am constantly in awe that he can be such a personal God to each one of us. That, too, is another amazing facet of his beauty.

There is one other aspect of his beauty I would like to touch on. In Revelation, John describes him as the *Lion of the Tribe of Judah*. I love this image. I see Yeshua as a Lion of all lions: majestic, kingly, powerful, strong, and always vigilant, ferociously protecting those whom he loves.

If I were to summarize this chapter, I would say that the beauty of Yeshua (I love that name!) is in his goodness. That one word captures it all. Goodness. All that he is. And all that he does.

Let me leave you with a verse which speaks volumes about the goodness of Jesus:

"Now it is an extraordinary thing for one to willingly give his life for even an upright man [one who is noble and selfless and worthy] someone might even dare to die. But God clearly shows and proves his own love for us, by the fact that while we were still sinners, Christ died for us." Romans 5:7,8 (AMP).

Chapter Thirty-one: The Beauty of our Multifaceted Savior

"Yet God sent us his Son in human form to identify with human weakness. Clothed with humanity, God's Son gave his body to be the sin-offering so that God could once and for all condemn the guilt and power of sin."
Romans 8:3 (TPT).

Since taking on the task of showing the beauty of Jesus, I have come to a place of feeling totally inadequate to do so. I cannot grasp the immensity of it. My humanity gets in the way. Yet I press on, doing my best with the help of prayer and his Holy Spirit. As is my habit, writing a psalm helps me to see more clearly:

A Psalm – Your Goodness

By Frank Curtiss, September 28, 2016

The entirety of the universe
  declares your glory, O God!
You have created a masterpiece
  for us to enjoy.
Your goodness surrounds me.
My mind cannot fathom
  the depths of your goodness.
My heart cannot hold

191

all the love you impart.
Your goodness envelops me.
You dwell in the highest heaven.
The stars are your footstool.
And yet you live among us.
Even within our human hearts.
Your goodness amazes me.
When my heart seeks you,
   you come near to me.
You fill me with awe and wonder.
I cannot help but love you.
Your goodness surprises me.
When the world catches me
   up in its clutches.
When I lose sight of you.
You gently draw me back.
Your goodness thrills me.
When I lose my way.
When I get lost in the darkness.
You come and find me.
You light my path to home.
Your goodness delivers me.
All your ways are perfect,
   O teacher of life.
May my soul seek after you.
May my parched soul be well watered.
Your goodness is like a spring
   welling up unto life.

I am in awe of all the many ways God shows himself to us. First, he shows us different faces within the Trinity: a wise and loving Father, a Son who came clothed in humanity to live among us, which makes God so much more relatable. And the Holy Spirit who takes up residence within us to be our teacher, our guide, and our comforter.

I am fascinated by the multifaceted ways in which God describes himself to us. I liken it to a prism of many colors. Each side shows us something different about his character. Within the framework of Father, Son and Holy Spirit, he describes himself as the King of the Ages, our shepherd, our Father, our brother, the Son of Man, the Lion of the Tribe of Judah, our healer, our redeemer, our comforter, our teacher and Rabbi, our judge, our High Priest (after the order of Melchizedek), our creator, and our husband.

He also uses metaphors, comparing himself to many animate and inanimate objects, each explaining different roles he plays in our lives to broaden our understanding of his character. He is our rock, our fortress, a sun and a shield, the bright morning star, our radiant hope, a spring of living water, the fountain of life, our defender, our strength, our sword, a Father to the fatherless, the potter, a gardener, our shelter from the storm, our shade from the heat, and our hiding place. This is only a partial list. I could write an entire book on this subject. Maybe someday he will call upon me to do so. He is full of everything that our hearts crave … lovingkindness, goodness, grace, favor, pleasure, and delight.

Essentially, the entirety of Jesus is beautiful … all of whom he is, his nature, his character, every single word he speaks, all of his plans, his every purpose. There is beauty in the riches of his Word, his wisdom, his perfect knowledge. Even his name—which we call *Jesus,* but is *Yeshua* in Hebrew and Aramaic—is beautiful. It means *"the Lord is salvation."* He is the one who laid out the plan for us to be saved—a plan that required his own beautiful suffering. It is he who courageously executed it. It is he who shows us the path, casting his own light upon it.

When Isaiah was prophesying about Yeshua, he wrote:

> *"But I will reveal my name to my people, and they will come to know its power. Then at last they will recognize that I am the one who speaks to them.*
>
> *How beautiful on the mountains are the feet of the messenger who brings good news, the good news of peace and salvation, the news that the God of Israel reigns!"* Isaiah 52:6,7 (NLT).

Yes, the very name of Jesus carries power. It also casts light. This week I was reading John, chapter one. I had difficulty getting past the first few verses because the riches are so deep. In it, I am seeing the beauty in the light of Jesus.

Have you ever been spelunking? I have. I remember descending deep into a Kentucky cave with a guide. When we were in its deepest depths, he extinguished all light. The darkness was so palpable I can still feel it. Then he turned the lights on and the beauty around us came into full view … the glorious stalactites and stalagmites. It was stunning. Later, we exited the cave into the summer sun … light so clear, so bright, so beautiful! It seemed more glorious than ever before.

I love the way *The Passion Translation* speaks it:

> *"A fountain of life was in him, for his life is light for all humanity. And this light never fails to shine through darkness—Light that cannot be overcome!"* John 1:4 (TPT).

There is breathtaking beauty in the light of Jesus which shines in the darkness. He is the Light of Truth, the full revelation of the Father, the Light of Life which lights our path, showing us the way to eternity. He is the light which can never be extinguished.

*****

Do you recall that I began by likening God to a prism of many colors? If you study light and what the human eye can see, you will learn that our eyes have three photoreceptors which capture three primary colors: red, green, and blue. These are not the same three primary colors you learned in art class. By mixing these three, we perceive the next layer, the seven colors of the rainbow. Some scientists who believe in God see the three primary colors as symbolic of the Trinity, and the seven as symbolic of the seven spirits of God mentioned in Isaiah and Revelation. I find it fascinating. Something I find even more fascinating is that the full spectrum of colors our minds perceive from these primary colors may be as many as one to three million. Yet there are birds and other creatures, including butterflies and bees, that have a fourth color receptor. Some scientists estimate that they may perceive up to a hundred million colors. My mind cannot fathom. Who knows? Maybe when we get to heaven we will have the ability to perceive all of those colors.

But let's talk black and white. Black occurs when our photoreceptors receive no input at all. White, on the other hand, occurs when we see a balance of the three primary colors. I find that rather fascinating when we consider that God is three beings in one. It makes me wonder … when we see all three as they are, in perfect balance, each fulfilling his role in our lives, do we see God more clearly? Is the light more pure? It's just a thought. There is one related idea to this: I have heard our pastor say that "there is no jealousy among the Godhead." I believe this to be true. When we speak highly of one, we honor all three.

Back to the first chapter of John. A little further down, he tells us, *"He [Jesus] has unfolded the full explanation of who God truly is."* John 1:18 (TPT). I think another way to say it is "He casts light upon all that the Father is." Jesus constantly desired (and still desires) to show us who his Father truly is. In my opinion, it is boundless. Even with the help of Jesus and the Holy Spirit, I doubt we will ever discover the fullness of his beauty on this side of the grave.

Chapter Thirty-two:
His Beauty Reflected In Us

The Russian author, Fyodor Dostoyevsky once wrote,
"Beauty is the battlefield where God and Satan contend for the hearts of Man." He was right.

"For everything comes from him and exists by his power and is intended for his glory. All glory to him forever! Amen." Romans 11:36 (NLT).

The way Jesus sees you and me is another reflection of his beauty. When he walked this earth, he did not shy away from those whom others considered untouchable. He placed his hand upon the leper. He offered words of eternal life to a Samaritan woman living in egregious sin. He healed the blind and lame beggars, and those whose demons drove them to madness.

The Word of God also has multifaceted words and phrases to describe all of who we are to him. We are a son or daughter, an heir, a servant, a royal priest, a holy nation, God's temple, God's workmanship, God's field, a child of the free woman, a child of promise, a bride, summoned, purified, forgiven, arrayed in a robe of righteousness, without blemish, full of wisdom, precious, and dearly loved. The list could go on and on. I am training my eyes and ears to see these things, and to make them a part of me.

A Psalm – Learning to Listen

By Frank Curtiss, June 27, 2019

O Yahweh, what would you speak to me today?
As I write, may your words flow onto the page.
May my heart hear your voice,
   and send it to my hands.
Quiet my soul before you.
"You are my beloved.
I chose you before I created the world.
I planned you as an artist plans a painting.
You began as an idea in my mind.
You are not perfect.
The beauty lies in the imperfections,
   those places where I continue to work.
For you are not finished yet.
You are like a sculpture,
   half emerged from the marble.
I see you as you are,
   but also, as you will be.
Yet even in your incompleteness,
   the hand of your creator is evident.
What was a worthless chunk of marble,
   cast aside,
     is becoming beautiful by my hands.
Stay humble and gentle my son.
For your beauty shines in humility.
It releases the light within you,
   allowing my goodness to radiate
     and be seen by all.

I know I have allowed you to suffer.
I looked on in sorrow
  at the broken spirit I had allowed.
But all of it is for my glory.
For my strength and beauty is on display.
And you will indeed rejoice on the day
  I reunite you with the ones you love.
Keep believing my promises.
For your every prayer is being answered."

I love something our pastor said recently: *"You don't want any thought in your mind about yourself that God does not have about you."* In my life I am trying hard to reset my thinking, to see myself the way God sees me. Sometimes, it seems to fly in the face of humility. Of course, it is true that we have not yet fully arrived into these things. But that does not matter to the Father. He always sees us in the best possible light. He sees who we are becoming.

I understand this better than I used to. Raising a granddaughter gave me fresh insight. Having raised four children and gone through the various phases of growth and development, including the challenging teenage years, I had a greater understanding of what to expect this time around. I found that I was far less likely to overreact. I could more easily see beyond, to see the diamond in the rough, to see the beautiful woman she is now becoming. That is how God is with us, only infinitely better.

Some of the ways that Jesus sees us are easy to grasp. Others are more difficult. In the chapters ahead, I will explore some of these. Especially those in which God is continuing to grow my understanding, such as my priesthood, and of being the bride of Christ.

Chapter Thirty-three: His Beauty Reflected All Around Us

A Psalm – Your Creation Amazes Me

By Frank Curtiss, March 19, 2019

God of all life
Your creation amazes me
It speaks of your glory
Words cannot describe it
This world is a miracle
Every cell held together
   by the power of your hand
Every tree, every flower
   springs forth because
     you set it all in motion
Trillions of things in balance
All held together by you
Yet this is the fallen version
The new earth will make this planet
   pale by comparison
The ravages of man
   will be evident no more
All will be right and good

Its beauty will astound us
We will have eternity to discover it
   and the galaxies beyond
All recreated
Designed by the masterful artist
Death will reign no more
Sorrow will be unknown
Joy will lead us to joy
Laughter will be born
   from hearts that overflow
Your goodness will permeate
   every crack, corner, and crevice
Come Lord, Jesus!
Come and be our King
Establish your everlasting
   kingdom of righteousness

God has instilled in us a deep desire, a hunger, a yearning for beauty. We spend a great deal of our time, energy, and money to surround ourselves with things that please our senses. I love to observe beauty. I also love to create it. I have a list I keep on my phone of the ten main values that drive my life. Creating beauty is just below loving God with all of my heart, soul, mind, and strength, and loving those he places in my life.

I love to create beauty in art. Oil painting is my favorite medium. I am a chef. Creating beauty with food is my passion. It is a gift from God with which I am able to bless others. I am a photographer. I love to capture the beauty around me. And I love to put words together in a way that will stir a person's soul. I am not a musician but am deeply passionate about beautiful music. I also enjoy beautiful architecture. My wife and I have been blessed to travel to Italy on three occasions. I walk around with my mouth agape, in awe of the ancient buildings and cathedrals, masterpieces of design, not to mention the art within.

As people, we try to beautify our outward appearance. We carefully select our clothing. We fix our hair and make-up. We hold in high regard those who excel in physical beauty. Some of us even get surgery, trying to enhance our beauty or hold on to the beauty of our youth. But none of this can come close to the beauty of our savior.

I've yet to touch on how the beauty of Jesus is reflected in his creation, those things he has given us to enjoy. He is a master creative artist. I believe that all of the best we see around us is a reflection of what heaven will be like. I love to ponder just how glorious it will be, beyond anything we have ever seen or imagined.

When Rhonda and I were in Hawaii a few months ago, I paddled a kayak across Captain Cook Bay to snorkel the reef on the other side. As I crossed the bay, I encountered a pod of Spinner Dolphins. A number of kayakers sat motionless in the water, not wanting to interrupt the incredible show they were putting on for us as they leapt high in the air, spinning like ballerinas as they did so. I felt like they were leaping for joy in praise of their creator. When I reached the other side, I entered an entirely different world beneath the surface of the ocean, where I was surrounded by hundreds of tropical fish and other creatures of every shape, size and color.

Earlier I described to you the glorious sunsets and double rainbows God blessed us with. I love that God's creation shows up on both a grand scale and in miniature. On a clear night, if you are able to get away from the artificial light, the stars and planets come alive to us. When I gaze upon the vastness of the universe, of which I can see only the tiniest portion, I realize how small and insignificant I am.

Here on earth, we see majestic mountains that leave us in awe. Here in Washington State, we have the massive Mount Rainier. We don't even call it by its name. We simply refer to it as *The Mountain*.

One love of mine are cumulus cloud formations that tower into the sky.

Having grown up at the beach, the ocean may be my greatest love. Its immensity and the beauty of its many moods hold an extra special place in my heart. I can sit for hours and watch the waves. I feel God's pleasure when I am there.

I love that the artistry of God's creative beauty shows up on a tiny scale, as well. Rhonda and I collect seashells, of which no two are exactly alike. Pearls are small but carry great value. When I spend time in my garden I get to see his artistic beauty in the flowers and vegetables I grow.

I could go on for pages about lakes and waterfalls, and an eagle soaring in the sky. This morning as I was writing outdoors on a beautiful spring morning, I was serenaded by several species of birds singing his glory together. But I think my favorite of all is seeing his beauty reflected in the face of a newborn baby (and in their baby fingers or toes). I doubt that I could ever adequately describe the immense joy I felt when my children and grandchildren were born.

On the other end of that spectrum, God has given me an appreciation of the wizened beauty which shows up near the end of our lives. To me there is something beautiful in the face of an elderly man or woman that reflects all of life's joys and heartaches. Here is one more psalm I wrote:

A Psalm – Magnificent in Your Splendor

By Frank Curtiss, March 9, 2020

Your glory, my Yeshua
Outshines the beauty of a sunrise on a bright morn
You are magnificent in your splendor
Is there anything I can compare it too?
There is much beauty in this world

All of it created by your hand

The beauty of the ocean on a clear morning

A glorious sunset upon the horizon

Or a baby's first smile

A beautiful woman of character

Or a crystal blue lake

A flower newly bloomed

The mountains in the setting sun

Or the stars on a black night

When you add it all together

It still pales when compared to you

All of it is a gift to us

Given for our pleasure

I can only imagine the glory of the next world

Crowned by the New Jerusalem

Magnificently perched upon Mount Zion

Make me an instrument of your love

Show me the path you want me to walk

That I might help this world

   to behold your beauty in all its purity

Chapter Thirty-four:
His Beauty Seen in the
Throne Room of Heaven

A Psalm: Awesome on Your Throne
Frank Curtiss, July 10, 2021

You are awesome on your throne O God
Your light radiating forth
Blinding me to all but your beauty
My selfish desires fall away
You dwell within me
A mystery unfolding
May my heart worship you forever
Because you dwell within
There is no escaping your love
It is forever within my soul
If I travel to the farthest ends of the earth
You are still within me
I will never be lost to you
Your love will never fail me
I will not dread old age
For it only draws me closer
One day I will see your beauty
Face-to-face, my eyes will see

Such compassion and joy in your own
I will fully experience your majesty
And cry out holy, holy, holy

Let's now explore a different aspect of the beauty of Yeshua—that seen in the throne room of heaven. I debated whether or not to include this. It is hard for my mind to fully grasp. But I feel that any description of his beauty would be incomplete without it. It creates a response in me which is different than any I have described so far. It inspires deep awe and reverence. That reverence is a good thing. It is a form of love that I believe is important for us to understand.

Let's explore the throne room now, as described in the book of Revelation, primarily in the fourth and fifth chapters. John the Apostle, while "in the Spirit," experienced a vision of heaven. He explains that he was invited into the throne room by an angel. This is a good time to engage your holy imagination once again. Let it help you visualize this scene as you meditate on its unspeakable glory.

When John arrives, the first thing that catches his attention is Yahweh, our Father God, sitting upon his throne. He describes his appearance as being brilliant as a gemstone—like the crystalline sparkle of jasper, which some say is like a diamond, and the fiery red of carnelian. I have heard it said that the red represents his passionate heart of love. Surrounding the throne is a rainbow. John likens it to an emerald, which was probably its dominant color, though it likely exhibited all seven of the colors of the rainbow.

If you think this is a placid scene, think again. There are violent rumblings of thunder and flashes of lightning. When Jesus speaks, his voice thunders like crashing ocean waves. In front of the throne seven lamps are ablaze, which we are told are the Seven Spirits of God. Before the throne lies an immense expanse that John described as looking like a sea made of glass.

In chapters one and two, we see Jesus among the lampstands. He is wearing a long, priestly robe with a gold sash over his heart, which represents his compassionate love for his bride. His hair is as white as snow and his face is shining like the brightness of the sun. His radiance speaks of his righteousness, his authority and his justice. His eyes flash like flames of fire in righteous judgment and his feet are like white-hot burnished bronze. John also describes a sharp, double-edged sword coming from Jesus' mouth, an image which speaks metaphorically of the Word of God—the sharp, two-edged sword.

As Jesus walks among the burning lampstands, he is holding seven stars in his right hand. These represent the angels of the seven churches he is about to address.

Can you imagine the scene? John, the same man who lay against Jesus breast at the last supper, is now so overwhelmed with awe and fear that he falls down at the feet of Jesus, as if dead. Then Jesus lays his right hand on him and says:

> *"Don't be afraid! I am the First and the Last. I am the living one. I died, but look—I am alive forever and ever! And I hold the keys of death and the grave."* Jesus goes on to tell John, *"Write down what you have seen—both the things now happening and the things that will happen."* Revelation 1:17-19 (NLT).

Now, returning to chapter five, we see two images of Jesus which seem in sharp contrast to one another. John is found greatly weeping. No one was found worthy to open the scroll with its seven seals. Then, one of the elders came to him and said, *"Stop weeping! Look closely, the Lion of the Tribe of Judah, the Root of David, has overcome and conquered!"*

The Lion of Judah was found worthy. In the very next verse, John gives us a very different image. In the midst of the four living creatures and the elders:

"I saw a Lamb (Christ) standing, [bearing scars and wounds] as though it had been slain, with seven horns (complete power) and with seven eyes (complete knowledge), which are the seven Spirits of God who have been sent [on duty] into all the earth."
Revelation 5:5,6 (AMP).

As the scene continues, we see the Lamb (Jesus) approach his Father and take the scroll from his hand. The twenty-four elders fall down before the Lamb. Each one is holding a harp and a golden bowl of incense, which we are told are the prayers of the saints … your prayers and mine.

The thing which strikes me most in this scene is the worship. Around the throne, the twenty-four elders, dressed in pure white with gold crowns on their heads, begin to sing. We also see four living creatures unlike anything we have ever seen, except that they have familiar faces: one like a Lion, one like an ox, one like an eagle, and one like a lamb. Each one has six wings and eyes all around with which they behold the glorious beauty of the lamb. Day and night they cry out *"Holy, holy, holy is the Lord God almighty who was, and is, and is to come."*

Surrounding them are myriads and myriads of angels, too numerous to count. These angels are joined by *"every created thing that is in heaven or on the earth or under the earth [in Hades, the realm of the dead], or on the sea."* All of them are worshipping God who sits on his throne, and the Lamb. All of them in unison are saying, *"To Him who sits on the throne, and to the Lamb, be blessing and honor and glory and dominion forever and ever."* Revelation 5:13,14 (AMP).

This scene is more than even my *holy imagination* can grasp. As I contemplated it, I felt God showed me something. I saw how this scene stands in sharp contrast to a scene we see described in the book of Daniel. There, the Babylonians, along with the people they had subjugated, were forced to worship the golden idol which Nebuchadnezzar had made in his own image. I'm sure many of you are familiar with the story of Shadrach, Meshach, and

Abednego, and how Nebuchadnezzar had them thrown into a fiery furnace when they refused to bow. The way God showed up in their midst to protect them is one of my favorite stories.

This scene in heaven is the complete opposite. God does not subjugate us. This worship is by free will, inspired by a burning heart of love for him because of all he has done for us. It is worship born out of deep reverence when we see all that he truly is—his glory, his majesty, his beauty, and the evidence of the unthinkable sacrifice he made for us. All who are present have seen the Father and Jesus face to face. And all they want to do is fall down and give their all to him.

I don't know how to finish this chapter, other than to once again say that I am undone by his beauty. As I behold it and invite it within, my heart yearns to see more of his beauty, and to have that beauty reflected in me.

Chapter Thirty-five: Beauty from Ashes

"And we all, with unveiled faces, beholding the glory of the Lord, are being transformed into the same image from one degree of glory to another. For this comes from the Lord who is the Spirit." 2 Corinthians 3:18 (ESV).

Wow! Read that again. It clearly tells us that when we recognize the beauty of Jesus we are changed. When we recognize his incomparable value, his superiority to everything else in all creation, we begin to look more and more like him. The more we desire him, the more he changes us into his image. How does this happen? It is a deep work. He begins with the heart. He works from the inside out.

A Psalm – The Lord Speaks Shalom Over Me

Frank Curtiss, January 23, 2023

The Lord, my rock on which I stand
Speaks over me …
"Shalom, you whom I love
I will multiply your peace
Your joy will erupt and overflow
Because you have chosen well
You have said, *"I will trust …*
I will place my trust in Adonai
For he is my mountain fortress"
I know this was no easy choice

On the day you faced adversity …
When your faith in me was tested
You chose to stand against the storm

Jesus loves to create beauty from brokenness. He gathers up our ashes and creates something beautiful—always different—always a reflection of his own beauty and goodness. We are his beautiful masterpiece; a work of art being lovingly restored by the Father.

One of the things that happens when we behold his beauty, his glory, allowing ourselves to be overwhelmed by it, it begins to remove from us the desire for the inferior pleasures of this world. This has been true in my own life. I used to work really hard at trying to overcome my sins. My attempts to manage the temptations that were my Achilles heel was agonizing. I would try, and fail. I experienced guilt and shame. It was a never-ending circle of frustration that only seemed to make matters worse.

God has broken that cycle in my life. In my beholding Yeshua, my love for him has become so powerful that it has broken the bonds of sin. Don't get me wrong. I still sin more than I should. But it is no longer my taskmaster. The more I behold him, the more I desire to be like him. Yes, I am becoming more like him every day. The desires of my heart are changing. Those things that once captured my attention have begun to release their grip on me.

What is the lesson in this? For me, it is to stop focusing on my sin. If we focus our energy on the beautiful one, allowing ourselves to be captivated by his beauty, the desire to sin will slowly ebb away like the tide. You may not even notice it until it has gone some distance.

When Jesus walked among us, he desired to do the things that the Father did and speak the words that the Father spoke. That is now my desire. And like those throngs surrounding his throne, the more I take in his beauty, the more I desire to worship him. He is worthy of my adoration. I have become intoxicated by his beauty. As we do so, he changes the very DNA of our hearts to make us more like him.

These changes don't happen overnight. I am sometimes surprised when I see young believers around me who are so much further along that path than I was at their age. But I do not begrudge them. I rejoice for them. I was a painfully slow learner. And I know that if God can make something beautiful out of me, he really must be a miracle-working God!

While I'm having fun at my own expense, I'll tell you about one of my favorite songs, a country song by John Anderson. The title and the lyrics start out … *I'm just an old chunk of coal, but I'm going to be a diamond someday.* I smile every time I hear it because it's true. Not because I'm anything special, but because God beautifies his people—he makes us sparkle and shine—even an old chunk of coal like me.

Even when I let him down, he still sees me as beautiful because love is the lens he looks through. He always sees his beauty reflected in us, always sees the best in us. His beauty creates beauty within us. Remember my favorite scripture from Isaiah 61? In the second verse he promises to, *"bestow on us a crown of beauty instead of ashes."* It is his work. Not our own. In the letter to the Romans, Paul encourages us with these words:

> *"So, we are convinced that every detail of our lives is continually woven together for good, for we are his lovers who have been called to fulfill his designed purpose. For he knew all about us before we were even born and he destined us from the beginning to share the likeness of his Son. This means the Son is the oldest among a vast family of brothers and sisters who will become just like him."*
> Romans 8:28,29 (TPT).

All around me I see the beauty of Yeshua reflected in his beloved. I see it in those whose countenance has risen from hopelessness to joy. I see it in people who at one time loved themselves first and foremost, transformed to people who now reflect his beauty with their love and compassion for others.

A Psalm —My Jar of Clay

By Frank Curtiss, March 7, 2020

Mahalo Papa
Thank you for your Spirit within
The divine living in my human heart
Held within my jar of clay
Where only ashes used to be
You took those ashes from me
You created something beautiful
You removed my stinking, moth eaten clothes
You bathed me in the blood of your son
And I came away pure
Clean and pure, from the inside out
A mystery
You placed a pure, shining white robe on me
The robe called righteousness
You set me a place at your table of delights
Joy now overflows my soul
Because I have believed your promises
My sorrow has been turned to hope
The sorrow is real and some will remain
Always there reminding me to hope … to trust
For that sorrow is only for today
Tomorrow, when I enter your presence
It will be forgotten·
I will dance the dance of a joyous bride
Who has wed her perfect beloved
Come soon my groom
I will swing the door wide for your arrival
I am ready and waiting in the night

God has a different path for each one of us to take to bring us to that place of beauty. The difficult truth is this: that part of our journey involves refining us in the furnace. None of us enjoy this. I sure don't. But it is true, nonetheless. And it is effective. The furnace burns away the dross in our lives.

David wrote, *"You have tested us, O God; you have purified us like silver."* Psalm 66:10 (NLT). Isaiah says it slightly differently, *"See, I have refined you, though not as silver; I have tested you in the furnace of affliction. For my own sake, for my own sake, I do this."* Isaiah 48:10,11 (NIV).

Notice that he states, *"For my own sake"* two times. I have to assume this is not an error in the transcript. He is making it clear that his refining of us—his creating beauty in us—is not for our sake, but for his. It brings him glory. As we become more beautiful, it makes him even more so—if such a thing is possible.

There are similar verses throughout Scripture. It is a hard reality few of us like to face. But none of us are exempt. Certainly, Rhonda and I were not. I wrote something earlier that bears repeating. I would never in a million years choose to walk through the losses we have walked through. They nearly crushed me. Nor would I wish them on anyone else. Yet, I know that God has used them to make us more like his beautiful Son. He was able to accomplish this because we did not turn away from him. And because he is faithful.

Let me leave you with one last thought:

> *"For the Lord takes pleasure in his people; he will beautify the humble with salvation. Let the saints be joyful in glory; let them sing aloud in their beds."* Psalm 149:4,5 (NKJV).

Chapter Thirty-six: How Do We Behold the Beauty of Yeshua?

"Let the beauty of the Lord our God be upon us, and establish the work of our hands for us; Yes, establish the work of our hands."
Psalm 90:17 (NKJV).

In the process of writing this book, I have asked God several questions. The first significant question was, "Why does the beauty of Jesus matter?" The question had hardly left my lips when he began to answer, giving me one insight after another in the days that followed. Much of it came through other people. Many answers came through his Word. Others came through his Spirit speaking into my heart. I wish all of my questions were answered so quickly! I can only surmise that he really wanted me to understand, not just for my benefit, but for yours as well. The same thing happened when I asked this question, "How do we behold the beauty of the Lord?" I knew the easy answers, but I knew there had to be more, and once again he began to open my eyes. The journey has been rich beyond my imagining. At times, it over-whelms me because there is no end to it.

Psalm: Blinded by Your Beauty

Frank Curtiss, March 22, 2022

Jesus, I am blinded by your beauty
By the pure light of your faithful love

Overwhelm every one of my senses

The best view of you is from my knees

May the things of this world fade away

Nothing on this earth compares to you

All that is good, true, and beautiful

Is a gift of your wounded hand

Wound my heart with your affection

Lead me into your holy temple

Let me gaze upon your face

Entranced by your eyes that search my soul

Ravish my heart Yeshua

Set my heart ablaze before you

A fire beyond my ability to control

May my eyes reflect the love you share with the Father

If I see you as you truly are

My heart will never be the same

If there is a role model for us in Scripture in this matter, it would have to be King David. What was unique about him that he would be so highly honored and called a "man after God's own heart"? He is one of my heroes of Scripture (I have many!). He was a man's man but had a tender heart towards God. He made huge mistakes but lived a life of repentance. He wanted nothing to stand between him and God. It is clearly evident in the Psalms he wrote and the life he lived. He was a *beholder*. The Lord was his delight and David loved to keep his eyes on him.

I love how this was made evident to us in Psalm 37. I am going to paraphrase this a little by adding three words in parentheses. I do not believe they change the heart of what is written:

"Delight yourself in (the beauty of) the Lord and he will give you the desires of your heart." Psalm 37:4 (ESV).

215

I see this verse very differently than I used to. I used to think that all I had to do was delight in God and he would be my Genie, giving me all the desires of my heart. That is what it says, right? That's a bit of an exaggeration, but you get the point. I was pretty sure he was not referring to my selfish desires … a big house overlooking the Mediterranean Sea, a Ferrari in the driveway. Those were not my true desires anyway. I knew then (and still do) that the truest desires of my heart are also his desires. The deepest yearning of my heart is that all of my family, especially my children and grandchildren, would walk with him, experiencing the abundant life he offers.

Over time, God has given me a new perspective. Now, the greatest desire of my heart is for him alone … to behold his beauty and his goodness. Those things cause me to delight in him, and he rewards me by giving me what I desire. It becomes like a circular equation. The more I delight, the more he gives of himself, causing my desire for him to grow ever stronger.

That does not mean I have given up my other desires. My loved ones are everything to me, but I know they are everything to him also. He desires the same things I do, probably even more than I do. And because it is his desire, as well as his promise, I grow increasingly confident that he will answer.

How else did David come to such a knowledge of God's beauty? First and foremost, he desired it. He asked God to show it to him. He sought God, and God answered. I am fully confident that God will do the same for you and me. He has promised as much, over and over. Jeremiah wrote, *"You will seek me and find me, when you search for me with all your heart."* Jeremiah 29:13 (NKJV). I can attest that he has kept this promise to me.

Seeking requires certain things of us. It requires that we *look* and *listen*. It requires us to take a place at his feet. There is no better place to watch and listen from. That is what Lazarus's sister Mary discovered, and Jesus honored her for it. I can picture her in a room crowded with other seekers, yet her eyes see only him as she listens intently to every word. To do the same, we need to quiet our hearts in his presence. That is a challenge in today's world, but not impossible. It requires that we escape the distractions so we can focus on him only. When we do, we can begin to hear the quiet voice of his Holy Spirit speaking to us. The Spirit he sent to guide us into all truth.

David had something to say about this, as well, in his very first Psalm he wrote, *"But his delight is in the law of the Lord, and in his law he meditates day and night."* Psalm 1:2 (NKJV). I invite you to read the rest of that Psalm so you can see the promise attached. The words that jump out at me here is *"he meditates."* He didn't just read it. He contemplated it. He kept it in his mind and thought about it day and night. What David referred to as the law was not just the laws of God, the Ten Commandments and the hundreds of other laws which surrounded it. It was the entire written Word available to him at that time. Essentially, he was meditating upon God, on his beauty and all of his goodness. He was contemplating what it told him about God and how God wanted him to live. It was so much more than a set of rules. It was about his relationship with the living God.

I am a huge advocate of spending time daily with the Lord in his Word and in prayer. But even that can become routine—with little life in it—unless we try to behold his beauty in the midst of it. For me, it is so much sweeter when I hear him speaking directly to me through his Word. After all, he is The Word, The Word which became flesh and dwelled among us.

I have my quiet places where I go to be alone with God. Before I open my Bible, I ask him to bring it alive for me. I ask that his Holy Spirit will fill me and help me see and grasp what he wants to say to me that day, and allow it to reach deep into my heart. My prayer is never exactly the same. I pray as the Holy Spirit leads me. But you get the gist of it.

I am passionate about the Word of God! So much so, that sometimes I get caught up in it and short my prayer time. I am working to find a better balance, but God has given me a sense of freedom. Rhonda and I try to practice the idea of prayer without ceasing. It's not that we pray every moment of every day, but when needs arise we often stop and pray about it right away. And I send prayers to God's throne room throughout the day as things or people come to mind. I believe David lived his life that way, devoted to a life of prayer. His prayers are interwoven throughout the Psalms he wrote.

Chapter Thirty-seven: Beholding His Beauty as We Pray

A Psalm – I Rejoice in Your Goodness

By Frank Curtiss, April 13, 2023

This morning I smile and rejoice
I rejoice in your amazing goodness
In the beauty of Yeshua my beloved
I do not always understand your ways
But I know you are always good
Even when I cannot see it
   you are working on my behalf
You have given me an open invitation
   to come and talk with you
Your arms of love are always open
You invite me to climb up on your lap
I smell your musky aroma
   mixed with the aroma of incense
The incense of my desperate prayers
Every prayer is precious to you
You love to talk with your children
You smile when we rejoice
Your heart weeps when we sorrow

You save our every tear in a bottle
They are not wasted on you
For they come from a heart of flesh
When our heart is soft like clay
   you mold it with your loving hands
You mix our tears with ashes
   and create something beautiful
A heart like your own heart
A heart which feels the pain of others
And laughs with them when they rejoice
I cannot help but love you
Even when I was angry with you
   you were oh so patient with me
You poured out even greater lovingkindness
You showed me the beauty of your suffering
How could I stay angry at a God who
   bore the weight of my sorrow upon a cross?
When my bones were dry and lifeless
   you spoke new life into them
You sent the wind of your Spirit
You breathed new life into my lungs
You took away my days of hopelessness
You filled my mouth with songs of praise
My tears became tears of joy!

I want to sidetrack for a moment to clarify something about prayer. We can get way too hung up on what some refer to as "prayers of petition"—bringing our own needs before God. The same can be said of intercessory prayer—lifting up the needs of others. These are important. They should not be neglected. But I believe they should be secondary to our prayers of adoration and thanksgiving—of beholding and worshipping the Lord in his beauty and goodness.

Another type of prayer not to be neglected are our prayers of confession and repentance. They cleanse our hearts and minds and keep our fellowship with him untainted. Let's face it. The pure white garments of our righteousness get dirty and we need to wash them again in his blood. I typically start my prayer time with prayers of praise and thanksgiving, but if he has already shown me something I need to repent of, that too can be a good place to start. I've come to realize how quick he is to forgive when I do. If I continue to feel guilt and shame after my heart has truly repented, it is not from him. You can guess where that comes from.

I don't know about you but I often feel inadequate in my prayers. I feel that they lack the faith and power to move heaven, especially those prayers that I have been praying for decades. But God is teaching me. He is encouraging me not to give up.

Let me share something he has impressed upon me. The Word tells us that Jesus himself and the Holy Spirit intercede to the Father on our behalf. I love that! In Romans, Paul tells us:

"In a similar way, the Holy Spirit takes hold of us in our human frailty to empower us in our weakness. For example, at times we don't even know how to pray, or know the best things to ask for. But the Holy Spirit rises up within us to super-intercede on our behalf, pleading to God with emotional sighs too deep for words. God, the searcher of our heart, knows our longings, yet he also understands the desires of the Spirit, because the Holy Spirit passionately pleads before God for us, his holy ones, in perfect harmony with God's plan and our destiny."
Romans 8:26-28 (TPT).

A few paragraphs later, in verse 34, we are told that Jesus, who had conquered death, was risen and exalted to the Father's right hand, is interceding with the Father for us. Knowing that the Spirit and the Son are praying for me gives me peace because I believe they know exactly what to pray. They know me better than I know myself. And they know what I will need to grow in my faith and trust.

Wow! This is amazing news. I don't feel pressure to get my prayers exactly right. And since they are already praying with and for me, I figure I might as well join them. I often ask Jesus and the Holy Spirit, "What shall we pray together today?" I find so much more freedom in my prayers when I follow their lead. They always have something to give, even when I don't. God shows up when I have nothing to give. When I fail to rely on him, there is little I can truly give. I confess that I do that far too often.

Let me tell you one more way I have found to live as David lived, constantly beholding the beauty of Jesus. It is in journaling and writing psalms. Not all of you will glom onto this idea. I know people I highly respect who never journal, and have never even considered writing a psalm of praise or prayer. All I can say is that these things have produced beautiful fruit in my own life. They help me to meditate on God. They help me to hear his voice, and immerse myself in his River of Life.

In my journal, I often write down Scriptures that jump off the page at me. As I write them down, I invariably see something in them that I had missed. A single word can expand how I see it. It helps me meditate on his Word so that it can make its way into my heart. I've already shared a lot about what my psalm writing has done for me. I'll summarize by saying it helps me to behold his beauty. For that, I am eternally grateful.

*****

I want to share one more lesson I've learned from examining the life of David. When David became King, he did not let it go to his head like his predecessor Saul did. He fully desired to keep God in his rightful place on the throne. I have learned some really cool things recently that I knew little about. It is regarding the Tabernacle of David. When David became the ruler of Israel, he set up a tabernacle on Mount Zion, right in the heart of his kingdom. His desire was for God to be honored above all else.

It takes some careful digging in Samuel and Chronicles to get the full picture of this. David's tabernacle was first and foremost a place of worship. It was no small operation. He employed 4,000 musicians who played all kinds of instruments, and 288 singers divided into twenty-four family groups of twelve. It is speculated that this was so that worship could take place around the clock, with each group singing for one hour per day. He also employed 4,000 gatekeepers—those responsible for the day-to-day operations.

The centerpiece in the tabernacle was the Ark of the Covenant, which had been brought there with great ceremony and rejoicing. The Ark had significance for them in ways we will probably never fully understand. It represented God, his law (the Ten Commandments were inside), and his mercy—for the Mercy Seat resided between the outstretched wings of the cherubim. At one time, the Ark had resided in the Holy of Holies in the Temple built by Moses, a place only the high priest could go, and only once per year. Then, after a series of unfortunate events (you'll have to do the research), it ended up relegated to a small village called Kiriath-Jearim where it remained for twenty years during Saul's reign. In 1 Samuel 7:2 we are told that during that time, *"all the house of Israel lamented after the Lord."*

Now the Ark was in a place of honor, in the midst of his people. It resided in a place where the people could approach God. I believe this was a prophetic image of what was to come.

So, what does this tell us about David? It tells me that God was the centerpiece of his life. Although God had appointed him the king of Israel, he knew that God was the one true King. He built his very kingdom around God. And during his reign, Israel thrived as a result.

It is thought that many of the Psalms which David penned were written in his tabernacle. That makes sense to me. We know that many of them were written as songs intended to be sung by the musicians. It is also interesting to me that many of the Psalms written by those other than David were written by men who ministered as priests in the Tabernacle of David. Asaph was one of those.

I believe that this place of worship was a reflection of the throne room in heaven, and as such it created a prophetic environment. Many of the Psalms written prophesied the coming of Yeshua with amazing clarity. Those who wrote them could behold his beauty as they worshipped day and night. What a glorious legacy.

Chapter Thirty-eight:
Betrothed to Glory

A Psalm: Capture My Heart Yeshua

Frank Curtiss, October 10, 2021

Capture my heart Yeshua
Steal it from all other lovers
Turn my eyes to your beauty
Make my heart beat as one with yours
Your blood course through my veins
Make every cell of my body
Yearn for you ... you alone
As a salmon gives its life to go home
May I die to self, so I may find you
I will swim against the currents
To find my home in you
My resting place in your arms
Held prisoner by your gaze
Captivated by the purity of your light
No worldly treasure compares
To the beauty found in your eyes
Make my heart burn for you
My secret hiding place
Is found under your wing
When you take joy in me
I am undone forever

I remind myself continually about the purpose of this book. It is a love story, the story of my walk with Yeshua, and those things he has done to bring healing and redemption to my life, things that have created a burning heart within me for more of him.

The Bible speaks of us in many ways. We are called sheep, and servants of the Most High. The Father calls us his children—adopted into his family, his own possession, chosen by him to be heirs of his vast riches. We are friends and brothers of Jesus. Most of those things I have known and understood throughout the years of my Christian walk.

But there were two things which God calls us that I had little understanding of until the last couple of years. The first is our calling as priests. The Apostle Peter, the one nicknamed *the rock*, writes:

> *"But you are a chosen people. You are* **royal priests***, a holy nation, God's very own possession. As a result, you can show others the goodness of God, for he called you out of the darkness into his wonderful light."* 1 Peter 2:9 (NLT).

The second half of that verse tells us quite a bit of what our calling as priests entails. With a little study you will see that we are a people called to minister *upward* to God, and *outward* to those around us, declaring his praises. I have come to accept this calling. It is a gift.

The other thing I had little understanding of was that of being called "the bride of Christ." That will be the focus of this chapter.

As a man, the idea of being called *a bride* didn't sound all that appealing at first. I'm a man. Call me a priest. Fine. Call me a warrior. I'll wear that mantle any day. But a bride? Hold on a minute. But that was what he calls us. And all I can say is, "Guys, we need to get over ourselves!"

The first references of us being his bride go all the way back to Isaiah. From there, it threads its way throughout the Old and New Testament. Paul wrote to the Corinthians:

"I am jealous for you with Godly jealousy. I promised you to one husband, to Christ, so that I might present you as a pure virgin to him." 2 Corinthians 11:2 (NIV).

But the main place we come to understand this is in the book of Revelation where Jesus' beloved friend, John, wrote the following:

"Hallelujah! For our Lord God Almighty reigns. Let us rejoice and be glad and give him glory! For the wedding of the Lamb has come, and his bride has made herself ready. Fine linen, bright and clean, was given her to wear." Revelation 19:6,7 (NIV).

That's us he is referring to, assuming you have believed that Jesus is who he says he is and accepted his gift of salvation. This might cause some of you a little confusion. How could we currently be called *The Bride of Christ* if the wedding has yet to take place? To understand this, we have to take a look at the ancient Jewish wedding traditions.

In the days of Jesus (and long before), there were two phases to the wedding process. The first was the *betrothal*. The betrothal occurred in a ceremony much like a full wedding ceremony. During a sacred rite, the couple became wedded in nearly every way except for the physical consummation. They took vows to one another. She was his and he was hers. They drank wine together to seal their commitment. It was a binding covenant. Faithfulness was expected. That is why it was such a big deal to Joseph when Mary showed up pregnant. If they were to be separated, it could only be done by divorce. Joseph was about to do so quietly, until the angel appeared to him in a dream and explained what was going on.

After the betrothal ceremony, a groom would leave his bride in the care of her family and return to his father's home to prepare a place for her, a room where the two of them would dwell. She had no idea when he would return but was expected to be ready on short notice when he did. His return would often happen in the middle of the night, when the groom and his entourage would come with a great, joyful procession.

Does any of this sound familiar? It should. It is a picture of Christ and his bride. When we come to Yeshua, giving our lives to him, we are essentially entering into betrothal with our beloved. We drink wine together in communion, sealing our covenant. Jesus, our betrothed, has now returned to his Father's house to prepare a place for us. When it is ready—according to the Father's timing—Jesus will return for us and we will be together forever more. That is when we will have the wedding ceremony spoken of in Revelation. Our marriage will become complete. What a day that will be!

I believe God has shown me something about this. Though this wedding ceremony will be for the entire bride of Christ—all of us at once—I feel that somehow it will be extremely intimate at the same time. I believe each one of us will feel like we are standing before him, staring into one another's eyes as we speak vows and words of love. How could such a thing be? Ask yourself this: how is he now a personal God and savior to each of us individually in a world of billions—hearing every prayer, seeing each tear, and speaking affectionate words of love over each one of us? If he can do that, he can make our wedding to him the most intimate event we've ever experienced. And at the same time, it will be in the midst of our eternal family.

After our marriage ceremony, be prepared to celebrate. I believe the Marriage Supper of the Lamb will be a feast to end all feasts! It will be a time of rejoicing beyond anything any of us have ever imagined or experienced. If it is anything like the Jewish weddings of old, it will probably go on for a full week. Maybe longer. Some even think it will go on for the entire thousand-year millennium which follows.

Several chapters ago, when I began to write about the beauty of Yeshua, I thought it was going to be a single chapter. It turned into seven. In the following chapter, we will explore another aspect of his beauty ... the beauty of his commitment to us—his betrothed. It goes so much deeper than I ever understood. But before I do, let me share one last thing.

A few months ago, I had the opportunity to do a Wednesday night teaching at our church about the Jewish betrothal and wedding and how it is an allegory of our walk with Christ. At the end of it, I spoke of the intimate wedding we would have. For that I wrote a vow, words that I could imagine (with my sanctified imagination) Yeshua speaking over his bride. These are not my words. They come from the Word of God—things spoken by the groom about his Shulamite bride in the Song of Songs. I have listed the verses in parentheses to show you where you can find these in the Song of Songs. As you read it, visualize yourself standing eye to eye before your beloved, Yeshua, dressed in your spotlessly clean, white garment. And let your heart take in every word of love spoken over you:

"Who is this, arising like the dawn, as fair as the moon, as bright as the sun, as majestic as an army with billowing banners?" (6:10 NLT).

"Let me see your face; let me hear your voice. For your voice is pleasant, and your face is lovely." (2:14 NLT).

"You are beautiful, beautiful beyond words. Your eyes are like doves behind your veil." (4:1 NLT) ... like sparkling pools in Heshbon ..." (7:4 NLT).

"Turn your eyes from me; I can't take it anymore! I can't resist the passion of these eyes that I adore. Overpowered by a glance, my ravished heart—undone. Held captive by your love, I am truly overcome! For your undying devotion to me is the most yielded sacrifice." (6:5 TPT).

"You have captured my heart, my treasure, my bride. You hold it hostage with one glance of your eyes, with a single jewel of your necklace. Your love delights me, my treasure, my bride. Your love is better than

wine, your perfume more fragrant than spices. Your loving words are like the honeycomb to me; your tongue releases milk and honey, for I find the promised land flowing within you." (4:9-11 NLT).

"You are my private garden, my treasure, my bride, a secluded spring, a hidden fountain ... a well of fresh water streaming down from Lebanon's mountains." (4:12,15 NLT).

Chapter Thirty-nine:
His All-Consuming Fire of Love

A Psalm – When I Look Into Your Eyes
By Frank Curtiss, March 3, 2023

Yeshua, my King, my bridegroom
You have made me lovesick
The fire in my heart rages
I become faint when I behold you
Weak with loving adoration
When I see your beauty
When I look into your eyes
And see your desire for me
When I behold your joy
As you cast your smile upon me
All else fades into obscurity
My heart skips like a gazelle
Like a dolphin leaping from the sea
For you are my beloved
The very breath in my lungs

Until recently I had little understanding of the Old Testament book known as the Song of Songs. The title of the book indicates it is the *song of all songs*, superior to any other. I was like "Okay. Why is this book here? What is the purpose of all of these graphic descriptions of love between Solomon and his Shulamite lover?" I just didn't get it.

Throughout my walk with the Lord, I have come to understand God's fatherly heart, love like that of an affectionate father toward his son, love that nurtures, love that abides, love that is compassionate, patient, and kind … agape love. I also saw the love that would sacrifice himself for us, even though we were a rebellious lot.

The Song of Songs exposes us to a different kind of love. Love that is intimate, love that sees such beauty that it unravels us, love that creates a deep yearning within—love that causes our hearts to burn.

I have received some excellent teaching on the Song of Songs in the last couple of years. I've been through a verse-by-verse teaching on three occasions and come away with a much greater understanding. It is about so much more than Solomon writing about human love and passion. This book goes beyond a love story between a man and a woman. It is an allegory—a parable—about Jesus and his bride. If we take that view, we begin to see the deep intimacy of his love for us.

The entirety of the Bible tells us about God's love for us and his desire for us to love him in return. But nowhere is it presented more intimately than in the Song of Songs. The subtitle for this book I am writing is *Psalms and Other Writings from a Burning Heart*. For years I have seen that our love for God is the most important thing. We are told to love him with all of our heart, all of our soul, all of our strength, and all of our mind. It is his first command to us.

What I have now come to see is that the more I understand his intimate love for me, the more I will love him in return, the more my heart burns for him. It is not something I have to make myself do. It is my natural response to his deep and abiding love for me.

A few chapters ago, I wrote about our beauty being a reflection of him. Let me state it again … every bit of our beauty as his bride is a reflection of who he is. And the more accurately we see him and his deep affection for us, the more we are changed into his image.

A side note on this. I am of the opinion that, as we are being transformed into his image, we are also becoming more uniquely ourselves. He made each one of us with unique personalities, talents and gifting. We are not always true to ourselves, as we try to fit in to this world and be accepted. Society tries to cram us into molds and shape us into something we are not. But as we mature in him, we begin to see ourselves through his eyes. He frees us to be exactly the person he made us to be. He chose us exactly as we were.

Yes, he *chose* us to be his bride. He chose us to glorify himself. We are chosen. We are set apart to be his for eternity. Not only that, but he chose us when we were still selfish and immature.

In Ephesians, chapter five, Paul gives us instructions for our relationships as wives and husbands. I always saw these verses through the lens of how I am to love my wife. That is one application. But there is another. Read it this time through a new lens, the lens of how Jesus loves you.

> *"And to husbands, you are to demonstrate love for your wives with the same tender devotion that Christ demonstrated to us, his bride. For he died for us, sacrificing himself to make us holy and pure, cleansing us through the showering of the pure water of the Word of God. All that he does in us is designed to make us a mature church for his pleasure, until we become a source of praise to him—glorious and radiant, beautiful and holy, without fault or flaw."*
> Ephesians 5:25-27 (TPT).

Verse 29 goes on to say:

> *"No one abuses his own body, but pampers it—serving and satisfying its needs. That's exactly what Christ does for his church! He serves and satisfies us as members of his body."* (TPT).

I hope you see what I'm seeing here. Jesus is *tenderly devoted* to us. He makes us *holy, pure,* and *clean.* He grows us up into maturity— *glorious, radiant, beautiful,* and *holy,* without flaw, faultless. Jesus loves us fully and completely even in our immaturity. His method of maturing us is to cherish us! Let me say that again. The way he brings us to maturity is to cherish us! He does all of this for his pleasure. It gives him joy to cherish us, and watch us grow and become more like him.

> *I am not inclined to do a comprehensive study of the Song of Songs here, but all that I have spoken of is illustrated in the relationship between Solomon and the Shulamite. In the beginning, she is less mature. She sees herself as unlovely and unworthy. Their relationship is about him meeting her needs, making her happy. But as the story develops, we see her change because of how much she is cherished. Listen to the words he says over her:*
>
> *"You are all together beautiful my darling, there is no flaw in you … You have stolen my heart, my sister, my bride; you have stolen my heart with one glance of your eyes, with one jewel of your necklace. How delightful is your love, my sister, my bride! How much more pleasing is your love than wine, and the fragrance of your perfume more than any spice! Your lips drip sweetness as the honeycomb, my bride, milk and honey are under your tongue."*
> Song of Songs, 4:7,9-11 (NIV).

And as she feels his love that cherishes her, she begins to give that love back. She sees the true beauty in this man. Read carefully what she says about him. It is clearly prophetic of our Lord, Yeshua:

"He alone is my beloved.

He shines in dazzling splendor yet is still so approachable—

without equal he stands above all others, outstanding among ten thousand!

The way he leads me is divine.

His leadership—so pure and dignified as he wears his crown of gold.

Upon his crown are letters of black written on a background of glory.

He sees everything with pure understanding.

How beautiful his insights—without distortion.

His eyes rest upon the fullness of the river of revelation,

flowing so clean and pure.

Looking at his gentle face,

I see such fullness of emotion.

Like a lovely garden where fragrant spices grow—what a man!

No one speaks words so anointed as this one—words that both pierce and heal

words like lilies dripping with myrrh.

See how his hands hold unlimited power!

But he never uses it in anger,

for he is always holy, displaying his glory.

His innermost place is a work of art—so beautiful and bright.

How magnificent and noble is this one—covered in majesty!

He's steadfast in all he does.

His ways are the ways of righteousness,

based on truth and holiness.

None can rival him, but all will be amazed by him."

Song of Songs 5:10-15 (TPT).

I don't know that I will ever fully understand the depths of God's love while I live in this body. But as I look back on my life, I now see it as a love story—a story of how he loved me throughout. He loved me when I was struggling with sin. He loved me when I railed against him because of the loss of my children. He loved me when my faith was shattered and I no longer trusted him. He loved me enough to walk me tenderly through all of those things. I am more mature now, more eager to please him, because my love for him has grown from a flicker to a roaring flame. Yet his love for me has always been the same.

To end this chapter, let's take a look at what he spoke to his people in the book of Hosea. This was written during one of the lowest points in the relationship between God and his chosen people—when, by all means, God should have turned away from them—for they had rejected him.

"I will make you my wife forever, showing you righteousness and justice, unfailing love and compassion. I will be faithful to you and make you mine, and you will finally know me as the Lord. "In that day, I will answer," says the Lord— "I will answer the sky as it pleads for clouds. And the sky will answer the earth with rain. Then the earth will answer the thirsty cries of the grain, the grapevines, and the olive trees. And they in turn will answer, 'Jezreel'— 'God plants!' At that time I will plant a crop of Israelites and raise them for myself. I will show love to those who are called 'Not loved.' And to those I called 'Not my people.' And I will say, 'Now you are my people.' And they will reply, 'You are our God.'"
Hosea 2:19-23 (NLT).

Chapter Forty:
Fanning the Fire in My Heart

"The Lord doesn't see things the way you see them. People judge by outward appearance, but the Lord looks at the heart." 1 Samuel 16:7 (NLT).

It is all about the heart. The Word of God makes reference to our hearts more than eight hundred times! God examines our hearts. He desires to occupy our hearts … fully. It is where an exchange takes place, his love for ours. It is where we come to understand his love for us. And it is where our love for him begins as a spark and grows into a flame.

A Psalm: The Flame
Frank Curtiss, November 7, 2021

The fire on my heart burns low
Like a candle burning down
Barely able to be seen
I feel no warmth from its flame
Yet it still burns upon the wick
Refusing to be extinguished
Even by the winds of trouble
Fan the flame with your love Abba
Place your torch upon my kindling
Make my heart a raging bonfire
Visible for all around me to see

May its warmth reach outward
Blessing all who come near
Who draw near your presence
Join my heart to your bride
Hearts that burn with passion
Make us into a mighty wildfire
Unable to be bridled by man
Ravishing the land with your love
Burning away all that displeases you
Renewing the land for your return

My desire is for a bonfire … burning out of control! Not just in me, but in all believers. When that occurs, true revival will take place upon the earth. David wrote:

"My love for you has set my heart on fire." Psalm 69:9 (TPT).

Paul, when talking about hope in the book of Romans says:

"And this hope is not a disappointing fantasy, because we can now experience the endless love of God cascading into our hearts through the Holy Spirit who lives in us." Romans 5:6 (TPT).

I love this. It is the Holy Spirit that delivers the love of God into our hearts. I was recently thinking about this and God reminded me that our hearts are the temple of his Holy Spirit. He also brought to mind what happened when Solomon built the temple of the Lord.

When the temple was completed, many thousands gathered from all over the land to celebrate and worship the Lord. Solomon led the people in a prayer, inviting God's presence to dwell within the magnificent temple they had built. The moment he finished, fire came down from the sky. It burned up the sacrifices and the glory of the Lord filled the temple. The glory of the Lord was so overwhelming, the priests could not enter. When the crowds of people saw this, reverence and fear fell over them. They bowed with their faces to the ground and worshiped the Lord, whose name, Yahweh, was too holy to cross their lips. Spontaneously they began to sing, *"He is good; his faithful love endures forever." 2 Chronicles 7:3 (NIV).*

I love this story! In it, I see an allegory regarding our own hearts. Within the temple stood a brazen altar. It was the job of the priests to make sure that the fire on the altar never burned out. God desires the same of our hearts. He desires to fill our hearts with his glory, and that the fire of our love upon the altar will never go out.

Fire does many things. It refines, it burns away chaff, it purifies our hearts like silver. But fires must be tended to. The flame is the work of the Holy Spirit. It is our job to tend the flame, just as the priests had the job of keeping the fire burning. If we fail to do so, we may find ourselves among those of whom it is written, *"The love of many will grow cold."* Matthew 24:12 (NKJV).

Keeping the flame alive is not an easy thing. Culture dulls our heart. Many, many voices try to distract us. It takes effort to keep our eyes fixed on Jesus. We are to be a presence-centered people, focused on the One who is beautiful in every way. His fellowship, his presence, is always available to us. He will never turn away those who are hungry for him.

It is not about knowledge. Knowledge is a dangerous thing without relationship. It is about hearts eager for his presence and willing to go to the source to find it, the Fountain of Living Water.

A Psalm: Yeshua Come Light a Fire

By Frank Curtiss, May 2, 2022

Yeshua come
Light a fire
Deep within my soul
Burning hot with the passion

of your deep, deep love
Your love which calls
  to my deepest places
Invite me to come
  come to your secret place
Carry me there
  upon your shoulders
Place me upon the rock
Sit with me by the sea
Let us enjoy your creation
  together while we talk
The ocean of many moods
It is as vast as your affection for me
The sky above us never ends
Yet your glory fills its every corner
Not a grain of sand
  came into being without you
I cannot grasp such wonder
Yet as we sit her together
  your focus is on me
Attentive, caring, listening
To my deepest desires
What can I say?
How can I engage
  with the King of all kings?
But you treat me
  with such great affection
My heart is undone
Joy wells up within me,
  it overflows
  into the River of Life
  which flows to the sea
My heart is at peace

So how do we keep our fire burning? We provide it with fuel. Self-sufficiency will get us nowhere in the Kingdom. The more we mature, the more we realize our dependence on him. I recognize that I am insufficient. I know that I am fully dependent upon Jesus and his Holy Spirit. I see my need for the Word of God, and the fellowship of the saints. I provide fuel for my fire through reading his Word, gazing upon his beauty with a worshipful heart, fellowshipping with him in prayer, and fellowshipping with his people, who strengthen and encourage me. I believe it is impossible to go on this journey alone. I have never seen anyone withdraw from God's people and keep their fire burning strong. We need one another.

So, together, let us eat, drink, and feast on Jesus in the Word. Let us listen carefully for his voice which sets our hearts ablaze. He has given us his Holy Spirit to give us revelation and understanding. And may we never forget to keep our eyes focused on the beauty of his sacrifice.

Chapter Forty-one:
Ascending the Hill of the Lord

"But for those that fear my name, the Sun of Righteousness will rise with healing in his wings. And you will go free, leaping with joy like calves let out to pasture." Malachi 4:2 (NLT).

What a beautiful word picture. I think we downplay the fear of God. I am not one to go around quaking in my boots, fearing he will smite me every time I make a mistake. That is not the kind of fear I am talking about. The God I know only wants what is best for me. When he disciplines me, it is for my own good, out of a heart of immense love. Read Hebrews, chapter 12, if you don't believe me. He does this because his desire for me is to live a rich, joyful, abundant life, filled with hope.

I compare the idea of fearing him with the way children look up to a loving earthly father. They recognize that he is older and wiser. They realize that he always wants what is best for them, and if he chooses to discipline them it is for their own good, to teach them right from wrong. A father's love brings wisdom. It brings a sense of security. That is why Malachi says, *"you will go free, leaping with joy."* Oh, how we have lost this in our society and we are paying a dear price for it. There is little fear or respect of God, or for authority of any kind. It has led to lawlessness. I also believe it is one of the reasons we are facing a mental health crisis. People are happier and more well-adjusted when there are healthy boundaries. We feel loved. God knows this.

David asked a question in Psalm 24: *"Who may ascend into the hill of the Lord? Or who may stand in His holy place?"* Then, inspired by the Holy Spirit, he provides the answer:

"He who has clean hands and a pure heart, who has not lifted up his soul to an idol, nor sworn deceitfully. He shall receive blessing from the Lord, and righteousness from the God of his salvation." Psalms 24:3-5 (NKJV).

It is my desire to ascend the *"hill of the Lord,"* to go up to his holy place and worship him with those who love him without abandon. I am not a perfect man. None of us are. But we all have access to a pure heart through the cleansing of Jesus' blood.

I believe there is a gift to us in the fear of the Lord. It is called repentance. Many see repentance through the wrong lens. They see it as feeling guilty and that they must perform penance to atone for their sins. But repentance is a blessing. It is simply changing our heart so that we come into agreement with what God desires for us. It is a constant *keeping the slate clean* so there is nothing which interferes with our relationship with him. If we make repentance a lifestyle, we never have to walk about in guilt or shame, or go about worrying if God is unhappy with us. But without repentance, grace is of little value to us.

I heard our pastor recently say that we ought to repent when we put our hope in "something" as opposed to "someone." I loved this. It is so easy to look for our worth and security in other places. And we need to be prepared to repent of our attitudes and wrong thinking as quickly as we do of our disobedient actions.

David modeled repentance so well. With Bathsheba, he made a horrendous mistake. Not only did he sleep with her, but then he tried to cover it up by having her husband killed. I'm sure he saw his sin right away but was unwilling to face it until confronted by the prophet Nathan. All of us avoid confronting our sins at times. Our favorite tactic is to justify our actions and attitudes to ourselves, to God, and others. It's a miserable place to be. But the sooner we admit our wrongdoing, the sooner we can get back to a place of peace and joy. David repented openly and publicly. His repentance is recorded in Psalm 51:

> *"Create in me a pure heart, O God, and renew a right spirit within me. Do not cast me from your presence or take your Holy Spirit from me. Restore to me the joy of your salvation and grant me a willing spirit to sustain me."* Psalm 51:10-12 (NIV).

To truly understand God, we must be willing to see all sides of his character: his grace and his judgment; his mercy and the way he calls us to righteousness through repentance; his love and his hatred. Yes, there are things God hates. Proverbs chapter six gives us a list: haughty (arrogant) eyes, a lying tongue, hands that shed innocent blood, a heart that devises wicked schemes, feet that are quick to rush to evil, false witnesses who pour out lies, and a man who stirs up dissension among his brothers. I believe, based on the entirety of Scripture, that it is not the people he hates, it is their deeds.

When I read the gospels, looking at the words Jesus spoke, I see clearly that he loves forgiveness and hates it when we are unwilling to do so. He went so far as to say that if we do not forgive others, the Father will not forgive us. It sounds harsh, but our Father knows the destructiveness of unforgiveness in our lives, and in the lives of those we fail to forgive.

All of this said, I do not serve him out of fear, nor out of a sense of duty. I serve him out of love. I believe that when we serve him because we love him, it is pure joy. We do not feel burdened. We do not get burned out. We see him smiling over us and we feel his joy in us.

In the past, I served him out of a sense of duty, trying to please him and others. It takes all the fun out of it. Now, if I find myself in that place, I know it is time to take a step back and return to a place at his feet, that place Mary loved so much. As we stop and behold his beauty once again, it refreshes our souls, and we are ready to ascend higher up the mountain.

As I was pondering this idea of serving him out of love and desire instead of compulsion, it reminded me of the freedom we have in Christ. A few months ago, I heard a message about how our names have prophetic meaning in our lives. If you don't believe it, look through the Word and you will find dozens of examples. I decided to look up my name because I could not recall what it meant. Frank means *free*, or *free man*. It also speaks of *frankness*, as in being free to speak honestly. In the days that followed this discovery, it seemed like everywhere I turned in the Word of God it spoke of my freedom in Christ, freedom from sin, and freedom from fear. I am choosing to embrace it fully.

Yet, in my freedom I have chosen to become a servant, a bondservant of Yeshua. A bondservant is one who has been awarded their freedom, yet they choose to continue being a servant because they serve a loving master who cares for them. In my younger days, I was a slave to sin. It controlled me. Jesus has set me free. He healed my broken heart. He filled me with his joy and peace beyond my ability to comprehend. Now, I choose to submit that freedom to his will. He is beautiful in every way. I love him more than life.

Chapter Forty-two: Broken Vessels

A Psalm: A Million Pieces

Frank Curtiss, November 15, 2022

When God allowed my heart
To be shattered in a million pieces
I considered it beyond repair
I thought I would never again know joy
Never again feel the warmth of his love
Hope was a fleeting illusion
Never again to be captured
I looked upon the pieces
Scattered upon the ground
And grieved the deepest grief
For a great wind had arisen
And blown away all of the chaff
Little of what had been remained
I hid my face and darkness fell upon me
But God would not relent
He chased me until I collapsed
He held me down like a lion over fallen prey
I screamed at him for all the wrongs,

I believed he had done to me
I wrestled hard against his love
Until no strength remained in me
I am now a beautiful broken vessel
Perfectly imperfect
Unable to resist the power of his love

One of the things I love most about God is that he uses broken vessels. The vase he made on the potter's wheel (my life), has been broken and put back together multiple times. There are irreparable cracks and missing pieces. I could choose to see my vessel as one of no value, cracked and broken beyond repair. It would be easy for me to spend my energy looking backwards, living a life of guilt, regret, and shame. I still go there sometimes. That is where the enemy, Satan, would love to keep me. He tries to invade my mind with those thoughts. So, who do I believe? To let those thoughts take residence in me is to deny the power of God's love to restore us. And so I choose to listen to his Holy Spirit instead, and the truths he speaks over me through his Word. I acknowledge that I am a Royal Priest, called to minister to God and the people he puts in my life. God has no problem using my broken vessel. I believe he prefers it, actually. He fills my vase with his Holy Spirit and it leaks out all over the place. I find joy and freedom in that.

It has been eleven years now since the death of our daughter Jenna, and more than eighteen since we lost Joel. Not a single day goes by that I don't grieve their loss. The pain remains, but it is overshadowed now by joy and hope. God has given me faith—built on trust—that I will spend eternity with them.

Our lives are extremely rich these days. Our granddaughter arrived home from college for the summer, having finished her freshman year at Santa Barbara City College where she is studying art and art history. Like many teens, she struggled through the COVID-19 pandemic and the way it interrupted her high school years. She has come so far. Last summer we celebrated her high school graduation with a trip to New York, where she dragged us to all of the art museums. Art is her passion. We are so proud of the young woman she has become and is becoming.

My wife, Rhonda, a broken vessel herself, has blossomed into a courageous leader of women. She leads a Women's Bible Study at our church. She is highly respected among her peers because of her kindness, compassion, and steadfast spirit. We also host a church Bible study group in our home.

God has blessed my life in ways too numerous to count. It makes my head reel. I am known as one who brings men together. It is who God made me to be. I was recently given the opportunity at church to teach for four Wednesday evenings on *The Beauty of Jesus,* something our pastor asked me to do after hearing all that God was showing me. I was deeply honored, especially considering that he is the one who set me on that path of discovery.

Rhonda and I are blessed with good health and an abundance of friends who enrich our lives. And if you didn't figure it out already, we love the church God has called us to. It is thriving because of our pursuit of God's presence.

In every circumstance—in times of joy, and in times of pain— Jesus is making a new creation out of us, one which resembles his beautiful son. We are becoming his image bearers. I, for one, am choosing to see things the way David saw them when he wrote:

"You have turned my mourning into dancing. You have taken away my clothes of mourning and clothed me with joy, that I might sing praises to you and not be silent. O Lord my God, I will give you thanks forever!" Psalm 30:12 (NLT).

Chapter Forty-three: How Should I Then Live?

"This is what the Lord says: 'Stand at the crossroads and look; ask for the ancient paths, ask where the good way is, and walk in it, and you will find rest for your souls.'" Jeremiah 6:16 (NIV).

I have chosen the ancient pathway, and in it I have found a place of rest for my soul. Still, in the midst of all my blessings, I continue to ask myself an all-important question … How should I then live? I ask this question often. I stole the question from a book title, *How Should We Then Live?* written by Francis Schaeffer. I've not even read the book, though we once sat through a video series about it in our Calvary Chapel days. Yet the title has always stuck with me. I replaced *we* with *I* because it is not my job to tell you how to live. It is my job to live rightly before God. If I do so, I hope it will inspire others to do the same. So, I am speaking to myself in this chapter, reminding myself how I should live my life before God. You decide for yourself what you want to apply to your own life.

Part of the answer for me lies in the verse I showed at the beginning of this chapter. It is not about reinventing the wheel … or our faith. What was true hundreds, even thousands, of years ago is true today. God still wants me to live by faith. He wants my heart to trust him. He has gone to great lengths to earn that trust. He wants me to see that he is good.

To the Romans, Paul wrote:

> *"Because of our faith Christ has brought us into this place of undeserved privilege where we now stand, and we confidently and joyfully look forward to sharing God's glory."*
> Romans 5:2 (NLT).

Undeserved indeed! Yet there it is. It is where I feel my life has brought me. But if I want to lay hold of more of it, I have to begin with those first four words, *"Because of our faith."* Faith is one of the most foundational precepts of the Bible. I have some. I want more. I know it is important to my Abba Father.

I used to constantly doubt my level of faith. Now, I see it has been enough to bring me this far on my journey. In hindsight, I see that I truly have come a long way, and endured so much. And God is growing greater faith in me ... it is what he does. And it is because I have desired it. He always honors such desires. The process feels painfully slow sometimes. Later on, in that letter to the Romans, Paul asked them a question:

> *"What should be our proper response to God's marvelous mercies?"* His answer, *"Surrender yourselves to God to be his sacred, living sacrifices. And live in holiness, experiencing all that delights his heart. For this becomes your genuine expression of worship."*
> Romans 12:1 (TPT).

I found myself having to read this more than once to understand what he's saying. *"Live in holiness."* Ugh! Sounds like a tall order. But what does living in holiness mean? First, it is to love him with my everything, and love the people he puts in my life. That's seventy percent of the battle. And oh yeah, I must not forget ... walk in faith. I believe that if I do those things, the battle for my heart is won and every other sinful desire becomes secondary. It becomes my joy to make him smile.

Then he writes, *"experiencing all that delights his heart."* What is he saying? I think I get it. God's heart delights to see me walking in blessing … his joy, the peace he gives, in the hope that he has for me. So, I choose to embrace those things, to bring delight to his heart, the same kind of delight I experience when I see my loved ones flourishing as they experience those things.

He goes on to say, *"For this becomes your genuine expression of worship."* I become a living sacrifice when I serve him from a place of love. It is my truest worship.

I believe it is easy to get confused about what worship is. On Sunday mornings, we worship in church by singing songs of praise. But worship is so much more than that. It is a continual lifestyle … a constant attitude of adoration, a constant belief and awareness of his goodness. The Word says about God, *"But you are holy, enthroned in the praises of Israel."* Psalms 22:3 (NKJV). When I praise him, I enthrone him as King of my heart, his proper place in my life.

Back to Romans. In the next paragraph, Paul continues:

"Stop imitating the ideals and opinions of the culture around you, but be inwardly transformed by the Holy Spirit through a total reformation of how you think. This will empower you to discern God's will as you live a beautiful life, satisfying and perfect in his eyes." Romans 12:2 (TPT).

I'm glad it is the Holy Spirit that does the job of transforming my thinking. All I have to do is put myself in a place where he can do that. I read his Word. I talk to him and listen for his voice. I go to church and seek wisdom, and seek to help others discover it. But I can only give away that which has been given to me.

I recognize, at this time in my life, that God has matured me a great deal. Part of me wants to deny it, thinking I am being humble in doing so. But that would only deny the transforming power of God's Spirit. That is actually an insidious form of pride. I know there is no room for boasting on my part because I believe that all that I am … all I am becoming, is the work of his hands. I love the way Jeremiah says it:

> *"Let not the wise boast in their wisdom or the strong boast in their strength or the rich boast in their riches, but let the one who boasts boast about this: that they have the understanding to know me, that I am the Lord who exercises kindness, justice and righteousness on the earth, for in these I delight,' declares the Lord."*
> Jeremiah 9:23,24 (NIV).

I am sixty-nine years old now and have five decades of walking with the Lord. It has been a *long and winding road* as the Beatles would say. I am retired from my career now but I have no desire to retire from serving God. I can see the finish line in the distance and it only makes me want to run the race with more determination. He has given me a burning desire to keep my eyes focused on Jesus, my prize, and finish the race strong.

One of the things he has now called me to is to be a spiritual father. I do not feel deserving of such honor but I embrace it, knowing that is what he wants of me. He has placed me in the lives of younger men who are trying to figure out their role in his kingdom; and in some cases, how to overcome the sin that so easily entangles them. What a blessing. He invites me to speak the words he speaks and do the things I see him doing. He has called me to be an encourager. That requires love. He has also called me to mentor and to disciple. That is a big responsibility, one that I do not take lightly. And yet, doing what he asks brings me tremendous joy and fulfillment. I feel like I have found my groove.

In these relationships, God has called me to be my genuine self. He has called me to live transparently before him and others. I hope I am. That is the main reason I am writing this book. I deeply desire that my story—both my failures and my victories—might strengthen someone else. He has called me to walk in courage. He calls me to walk in integrity, to be a man who is steadfast, trustworthy and kind. I do not always succeed, but by his grace I am growing.

But none of this matters unless I live my life with a heart on fire, a heart ablaze with love for him. In the end, before I cross from this life into the next, I hope that it is the one thing that remains visible for all to see.

A Psalm - Your Lips I have Opened

By Frank Curtiss, June 1, 2021

I spoke and said,
"Open my lips Jesus
   and I will declare your praise."

Then Jesus spoke to me,
"Your lips I have opened.
Go and tell my praises
   to those who love me,
   and to those who seek, but
   have yet to find me.
I have blessed you with a story to tell,
   a story of tragedy,
   a story of redemption,
   of promises fulfilled,
   and promises yet to pass;
   yet seen from a distance.
Impart hope my son.
For I have made you
Trust in me again.
Bestow peace.
For I have opened your eyes

to see the mighty works
   accomplished by my right hand.
Take heart, my child, take heart.
For I am healing your broken spirit.
I am turning your sadness to joy.
This is the work of my spirit.
No man could accomplish this.
No amount of effort
   could bring this to pass.
But I am doing this,
   for I have loved you
   with a great love.
I have felt your pain.
I have placed a burning coal to your lips.
That words of slander and despair,
   should never pass by them again."

*****

Are you familiar with the account in Luke of when Jesus met the two disciples on the road to Emmaus? It took place just days after his death on the cross. These men were downcast as they walked along, talking about all of the things that had taken place. Their great hopes had died on the day Jesus was laid in the tomb.

As they journeyed, the resurrected Jesus himself came along and began walking with them. We are told that their eyes were prevented from recognizing him. Then Jesus asked them, *"What are you discussing together as you walk along?"* They stopped and looked at Jesus like he came from another planet, their broken hearts clearly evident. The one named Cleopas answered, *"Are you the only one visiting Jerusalem who does not know the things that have happened here in these days?"* (quotes from NIV).

Jesus played along. *"What things?"* he asked. They then explained all about his crucifixion and about how some of the women had reported going to the tomb on the morning of the third day and finding it empty. They did not know what to think of these reports.

Then Jesus said to them, *"How foolish you are, and how slow to believe all that the prophets have spoken! Did not the Messiah have to suffer these things then enter his glory?"* Then, beginning with Moses and all the prophets, he explained to them what was said in all the Scriptures concerning himself.

As the three of them approached the village, Jesus acted as if he would continue on, but they convinced him to stay with them for the evening. Later, as they were reclining at the table together, Jesus broke the bread and blessed it. Suddenly, their eyes were opened and they recognized him, but he disappeared from their sight.

Now, my favorite part of the story. They asked one another, *"Were not our hearts burning within us while he talked with us on the road and opened the Scriptures to us?"*

This is my desire. To hear the voice of the beautiful one with a heart that burns within me. Someday, I will walk by his side. Oh, what a day that will be.

Chapter Forty-four:
The Coming Reunion

A Psalm – The City of God

By Frank Curtiss, April 8, 2023

The City of God looms in my mind
My heart sees its majestic citadel
Rising high above all the earth
Glorious, majestic, perfect in beauty
The light of God's radiance shines outward
Illuminating every corner of the earth
The earth now restored to perfection
Untarnished by the sin of man
A perfect reflection of God's glory

Every now and then, when my faith is feeling weak, I ask God if he will give me another double rainbow as a reminder of his goodness. He has been faithful to do so … graciously reminding me of his goodness.

I mentioned earlier in the book that Rhonda and I traveled to the Big Island of Hawaii to celebrate our fiftieth wedding anniversary. A couple of the days were really rainy. The opposite side of the island had it way worse—like Noah and the flood worse. Hilo had eleven inches of rain in a single hour! I can't imagine.

On that Saturday evening, after we had not seen the sun all day, it dipped below the clouds at sunset, providing a glorious tropical sunset. I stood admiring it for a few minutes. Then I turned around and looked to the east—and yes—you guessed it, another double rainbow. Every person I could see had stopped to look on with wonder at the beauty of God's artistry.

The next morning, we attended a church near Kona. The stone chapel is small, so they have additional seating outdoors by the sea, with the service simulcast on large screens. The rain was gone. It was a fresh and beautiful Hawaiian morning.

As worship began, the first song they sang was called the "Goodness of God." I choked up with tears of gratitude as we began to sing about his mercy, goodness, and faithfulness.

*****

Throughout the greater part of my life, I feared death. I think most of us do. That is no longer the case for me. There are several reasons why that changed for me.

One, is that I have fallen deeply in love with God and his Son. I long to crawl up onto my Father's lap for a hug. I long to embrace Jesus and sit with him for a talk. I can't wait to look deep into those eyes of love.

The next reason is that there are so many people I love that have gone ahead of me, that I deeply desire to be reunited with. Don't misunderstand me. I have every desire to be around here as long as I can. God has given me purposes, reasons to be here. I have told you about my desire to be here for our children and grandchildren as long as possible. Not to just be alive, but to be healthy and engaged, able to be a blessing which enriches their lives.

That is one reason I exercise and try to eat healthy. I went cycling this morning with a couple of friends. It was a gorgeous spring day. We rode a loop that took us across Lake Washington twice. We crossed the lake on one of two floating bridges, and returned on the other. It was pure bliss to enjoy God's creation with these friends, while keeping ourselves healthy in the process.

It is not only the exercise that is healthy but the relationships. These friends ride for the same reasons I do.

Another reason I do not fear death is because I have taken a close look at what the Bible tells me about heaven, and of the New Heaven and New Earth to come, spoken of in the book of Revelation and other places. Many people do not desire heaven because they don't understand how truly amazing it will be. The church teaches little about it. I hear people say that their loved ones have gone to a "better place" and I want to grab them and shake them. That is the most understated statement in the history of understatements! It will be amazing beyond our ability to grasp. I love what Paul says in Romans:

> *"I am convinced that any suffering we endure is less than nothing compared to the magnitude of the glory that is about to be unveiled in us. The entire universe is standing on tiptoe, yearning to see the unveiling of God's glorious sons and daughters!"* Romans 8:18,19 (TPT).

Trust me, we won't be floating around on clouds like little fat cherubs playing harps. Nor will we be around the throne worshipping forever, and ever, and ever. I believe there will be plenty of worship, and I think a lot of it will be spontaneous. But God has so much more planned for us.

Another reason I do not fear death is he has personally given me visions of heaven. I suspect he's done this because of all that we have been through with the loss of our children. He knew my heart needed courage and comfort. Two of these visions stand out clearly. The images are burned into my memory so strongly that they feel as real as any actual event I have experienced. I will do my best to describe them, though I know my words will fall short.

I love Italy. It is a land blessed with rolling hills, rich earth, beautiful vineyards, and ancient hilltop towns. The reason I tell you this is because the first of my visions feel like such a place, only many times more glorious. In it, I find myself tending to my vineyard. Perched on the hill behind me is my dream home, built of solid stone, overlooking my vineyards, fields, and orchards, lush with fruit and other produce. The River of Life glistens in the morning sun as it flows through the valley below, coming from the New Jerusalem, shining like a radiant jewel in the distance.

That is just the backdrop. It's a perfect morning. I can feel the warm sun on my face as it evaporates the morning mist. Then I hear the sound of laughter. I see my daughter and granddaughter joyfully working side by side in the garden near a beautiful pool of water fed by a waterfall. I see my son, Joel, doing a cannonball into the crystal-clear water.

I hear footsteps and turn to look. I see Jesus is making his way up the hill with an affectionate smile on his face. He embraces me, then makes his way to greet my children and grandchildren. The girls grab a hose and squirt him. Can you imagine? Squirting the Son of God! But the next thing I know he grabs hold of the hose and is dousing them. Oh, what a scene. So unlike anything I ever would have imagined. The thing that stands out to me is the laughter and the pure, spontaneous joy!

*****

As if this were not enough to sustain me, several weeks later the Holy Spirit gifted me with a second vision. But first, let me give you a little background. I love music, and I've always wanted to learn how to play the guitar. The problem is, I have no musical talent. Thankfully, God has given me many other artistic gifts, so I have tabled it for now. But I've made my request known to God. When I get to heaven, I want my son Joel to teach me how to play the guitar.

I related the story earlier about the treehouse Joel wanted to build—like the one in *Swiss Family Robinson*—and how Jesus was helping him build it. These two things came together in my second vision. In it, Joel, Jenna and I are in the treehouse, and Joel is teaching me to play. As we are playing, the party begins to grow. Jesus shows up and joins in. Then, one by one, the other members of my earthly family begin to arrive: Rhonda, all of my sons, daughters, and grandchildren. It's a beautiful family reunion with singing, laughter, and hearts of deep gratitude.

Beyond the low bamboo walls of the treehouse, it feels like all of creation is hanging out with us. The tree is huge. As I look outward, I see panthers, lemurs, and other creatures reclined on the branches. They do not pose a threat because all of nature lies down together. And oh, the sky! The expanse is alive with swirling light and planets, a hundred times brighter than I have ever seen. All of it is synchronized in perfect harmony, glorifying him who created them.

*****

I have no idea if I will actually experience these things. These visions feel as if they came from God, but it is also possible they are just the work of an overactive imagination. Yet, this much I know for certain: that the place we know as heaven and the New Earth to come are going to be amazing beyond our wildest dreams. We know from God's Word that there will be no more sorrow, no more tears of sadness (but plenty of tears of joy), and no more death. And the focal point of it all will be Jesus, the Jewish man whom the Father has made anointed to be our King forever.

I love to daydream about our eternity. I wouldn't be surprised if God gave us another photoreceptor to see colors we have never seen, beautiful things we've never heard or beheld, and galaxies to explore. I envision people of every culture and from every historical age living together in harmony. In my sanctified imagination I see and hear music from every tribe and nation being played everywhere I go, all in worship to him who gave such talents. I can envision regular dinner parties at my home, overlooking my vineyards, lemon orchards and the River of Life. I can imagine inviting David and Jonathan, Moses and Aaron, Mary Magdalene, Isaiah, and all of the other saints I admire. Jesus will join us, and I believe each one of you at some time or another. After all, eternity is a long time.

One thing that blows my mind is the description of the New Jerusalem which will come down from heaven to the New Earth. It will be immense! The book of Revelation describes it as being fourteen hundred miles wide, and long and tall. Can you imagine a city that would stretch from Canada to Mexico? I have a theory that—because of its immensity—the New Earth will be much larger than our existing planet, with plenty of room for us all to spread out. Someday we will find out.

I also visualize each of us having a place of our own within the walls of this immense city, the New Jerusalem. In their early history, the Israelites made regular pilgrimages to Jerusalem to celebrate the many feasts God called them to. Each feast had a purpose: to remember miracles God had done for his people, like the Passover of the Death Angel in Egypt, or the giving of the Torah to Moses. I have a feeling these traditions will be resumed. Who truly knows, except God? I just know that whatever he has planned for us will be far greater than even my wild imagination can create.

Chapter Forty-five:
Tetelestai ... it is Finished

"Tetelestai!," the final word that Jesus uttered on the cross standing upon the hill of Calvary. *"'It is finished.' With that he bowed his head and gave up his spirit."* John 19:30 (NIV).

The Greek word *tetelestai* comes from the verb *teleo*, meaning, *to bring to an end, to complete, to accomplish*. It signifies the successful end to a course of action. It is a word you would use when you have attained a goal, when you reach the end of a journey, cross the finish line of a marathon, or the two-hundred-mile bike ride from Seattle to Portland. It means more than *I arrived*. It means *I accomplished exactly what I set out to do*.

It was also a word used in business, meaning *the debt is fully paid!* And a word used in judgment. When the judge said *tetelestai*, he was declaring that the sentence had been fully served. Lastly, it was used in a military sense, meaning *the battle has been fully won*.

Yet, there is more to be learned about this verb. *Tetelestai* is the perfect tense in Greek. It speaks of an action which has been completed in the past with results continuing to the present. It differs from the past tense which looks back to an event and says, "This happened." The perfect tense tells us that it happened and is still happening to this day.

These are the reasons my heart burns for him. He is steadfast and faithful. He is good. He is true. He is beautiful beyond my imagining. Lord, make my fire burn ever hotter. Make it an insatiable bonfire that everyone who comes near will see and be drawn to its warmth—your warmth.

I imagine if you've read this book, you are already a Christian, a follower of Jesus Christ. If by some chance you are not, but made it all the way through this book, I hope you are ready and eager to give your life to him. You will never regret it.

Not that the Christian life is a bed of roses. We don't get free passes to get out of the hard stuff. You have seen that in my own life. What we do get is a savior who is our comforter, our teacher, our best friend, and our beloved. And we get hope built on promises, the greatest of which is the promise of eternal life with him.

The path to becoming one of his followers is easy. All it takes is whatever faith you can muster to believe that Jesus is who he says he is—God's one and only son—one with the Father. Then accept the gift he is holding forth in his hands to you. Receive it with a heart that is willing to repent of the life you have lived up until this point. Betroth yourself to Yeshua. It will be the best decision you have ever made.

Here is one last psalm for now:

A Psalm – Watching Seabirds Soar
Frank Curtiss, July 23, 2020

My heart longs for you Papa

I long to take a walk with Jesus

To find a quiet place by the sea

To watch the seabirds soar

And the dolphins play in the waves

To sit and talk with he who created them

No friend is more loyal

You know me more than anyone

For it is you who created me

You know every noble thought

Every shameful thing I've ever done

And you love me anyway

You call me your friend

Your bride to be

At times I have doubted you

My trust evaporated like the morning mist

But you never stopped loving me

Even when I railed against you in anger

For you are the God of Compassion

You stood your ground

You let me pound upon your chest

As I screamed, "Why, why, why?"

When you hung upon the cross

A tear ran down your cheek

My sorrow became your own

You sent your Spirit to comfort me

To bind up my broken heart

And pour the oil of your love

Into my open wounds

Now I sit with you

I gaze into the sea and smile

A double rainbow shines above it

Your joy overcomes my heart

For you have never forsaken me

Nor those you have given me to love

Thank you for taking the time to read my story. I hope it has given you courage and strength. In it, I have told you a great deal about who Jesus is and have tried to impart his impassioned love. But know this, it is far greater than any single book can describe. Let me leave you with one last thought, the final verse from the Gospel of John:

> *"But there are also many other things Yeshua did; and if they were all to be recorded, I don't think the entire world could contain the books that would have to be written!"* John 21:25 (CJB).

May every remaining day you have on this earth be rich with hope, joy and peace. And if I do not meet you while we are on this earth, may we meet one another at the great wedding feast of the Lamb. Many rich blessings of love, joy, and shalom!

Biblical Resources Alphabetically:

AMP – Amplified Bible, copyright © 2015 by The Lockman Foundation

CEV – Contemporary English Version, copyright © 1995 by American Bible Society

CJB – Complete Jewish Bible, copyright © 1998 by David H. Stern

ESV – English Standard Version, copyright © 2001 by Crossway Bibles, a publishing ministry of Good News Publishers.

NIV – New International Version, copyright ©1973, 1978, 1984, 2011 by Biblica, Inc.

NKJV – New King James Version, Copyright © 1982 by Thomas Nelson

NLT – New Living Translation, copyright © 1996, 2004, 2015 by Tyndale House Foundation

TPT – The Passion Translation, a registered trademark of Passion & Fire Ministries, Inc. copyright © 2020 Passion & Fire Ministries, Inc

About the Author:

The Frank Curtiss is a retired restaurant owner. When his landlords sold their property to a developer, he decided to follow his dream of becoming a writer. This is Frank's first autobiographical work.

Frank and his wife, Rhonda, reside in Redmond, WA.

Additional Titles by Frank Curtiss:

Antonio Cortese Mystery Novels (in order):

Deception in Siena

Missing in Firenze

Death in Abundance

Cookbook: Paperback only

Frankie at Home in the Kitchen

Novels available in hardcover, paperback, and eBooks on Amazon. Autographed hardcover and paperback books also available on website:

www.frankcurtiss.com **(or use QR Code below)**